Maintaining Long-Distance and Cross-Residential Relationships

Maintaining Long-Distance and Cross-Residential Relationships

Laura Stafford
The Ohio State University

Routledge
Taylor & Francis Group
New York   London

First published by Lawrence Erlbaum Associates, Inc., Publishers

This edition published in 2011 by Routledge

Routledge

711 Third Avenue
New York, NY 10017

2 Park Square, Milton Park
Abingdon, Oxon OX14 4RN, UK

Routledge is an imprint of the Taylor & Francis Group, an Informa business

Cover design by Kathryn Houghtaling Lacey
Cover design concept by Jasmine Kuo

Library of Congress Cataloging-in-Publication Data

Stafford, Laura.
 Maintaining long-distance and cross-residential relationships / Laura
 Stafford.
     p. cm.
 Includes bibliographical references and index.
ISBN 0-8058-5164-x (c. : alk. Paper)
ISBN 0-8058-5165-8 (p. : alk. Paper)
  1. Interpersonal relations. 2. Long-distance relationships. 3. Separa-
tion (Psychology) I. Title.

HM1106.S753 2004
302—dc22   2004053285
                                                     CIP

Contents

Preface

During the early years of my academic career, I set out to study long-distance relationships. This pursuit was met with underwhelming support. I was advised to abandon such a foolish endeavor; long-distance relationships occurred so infrequently they warranted little attention. Being a pragmatist who desired tenure as opposed to an idealist who might thumb one's nose at such direction, I set aside this interest and continued along a path deemed more worthy. Less than 10 years later, long-distance relationships were identified as not only a significant relational and communicative phenomenon, but an understudied one at that (Wood & Duck, 1995). Within the last few years, the number of conference papers and dissertations on this relational form has increased substantially, though the number finding the light of publication remains limited; I anticipate this will change soon. Thus, I'm uncertain whether this volume is many years past due, or a very few years too early.

To the many people who have contributed to my worldview, I offer my thanks or apologies as each may deem appropriate. Also, I would like to acknowledge the input (at times demanded, at other times unsolicited and unwanted, though always needed) and support of colleagues, friends, and family (broadly construed) who endured me during the course of writing this text. The following supportive individuals, who are geographically proximal yet undoubtedly desired to be geographically removed more often than they expressed, warrant my appreciation: Martha Fay, Gene Frye, Julie Harden, Jeff Lerch, Bell O'Neil, Andy Merolla, Janessa Morris, Shuangyue Zhang, Artemio Ramierz Jr., Jason Stafford, Jeffrey Stafford, and Sean Stafford. Forgiveness is sought from the graduate students of my family communication seminar as they had the unfortunate experience of every discussion finding its way back to this project. Finally, heartfelt thanks are extended to members of my ballet class. They know why.

1

Introduction

Numerous individuals in the United States live apart from someone about whom they care whether lover, friend, parent, child, sibling, grandparent, or other relation. People may have long-distance relationships (LDRs) for a variety of reasons, such as educational or career pursuits, military deployment, incarceration, divorce, or simply growing up or moving away. In many cases, individuals have close ties to people who may be geographically close but who do not live together, such as children and noncustodial parents. These cross-residential relationships share similarities with LDRs in that access for day-to-day communication is limited. Given the priority granted frequent face-to-face (FtF) interaction to sustain close relationships, it is remarkable that the maintenance of geographically distant and cross-residential relationships has been given so little academic research attention.

Much of what we do know about LDRs and cross-residential relationships is not derived directly from studies on them. Rather, proximity and residential structures are often included as one of many constructs of interest in studies on family relationships or mobility patterns. Thus, for this volume, insights into these relationships are drawn from numerous disciplines including, but not limited to, interpersonal communication, relational studies, social psychology, family studies, media studies, military science, gerontology, sociology, and criminology.

Long-distance and cross-residential relationships occur in opposition to many U.S. cultural assumptions about the nature of communication and close relationships. Such presumptions especially relevant to LDRs include: frequent FtF communication is necessary for close relational ties; geographic proximity is necessary for relationships to be emotionally close; shared meanings are necessary for relational maintenance; and family members, especially married parents, and parents and young children, are supposed to share a residence. These relationships, and hence this text, challenge such assumptions.

The knowledge base on which this text is founded is not without limitations. Research on dating relationships, dual-career relationships, and young adult–parent relationships is based almost exclusively on Caucasian middle-class heterosexual samples. Studies concerning separation due to occupation, military deployment, incarceration, extended family relationships, and friendships come from a much broader racial and socioeconomic spectrum. The literature on cross-residential relationships predominately concerns the effects of the absent father, as mother absence remains understudied. Research on how family relationships are maintained and managed across residences is sparse.

Limited consideration is given to cross-national relationships, although 11.5% of the current United States population was born outside of this country (Schmidley, 2003). Intuitively, most of these individuals left behind family and friendship networks. Research on most international immigration is limited as its focus is much more on assimilation or adjustment to life in the United States than on ties with those in the home country.

It is not the intent to privilege one group or type of relationship over another. Rather, space limitations and the deficit of research in some areas dictate a relatively narrow scope. The following paragraphs outline the chapters to follow and offer a brief organizational overview of the text.

Chapter 2 offers a rationale for the study of LDRs and working definitions of critical concepts, and it overviews some cultural assumptions about relationships. Chapter 3 turns to selected theoretical orientations to the study of relational maintenance in particular and relationships in general.

Chapters 4 and 5 focus on romantic relationships, college dating relationships, and adults who are separated because of occupation, military duty, or incarceration.

Chapter 6 considers young children who are separated from one or both parents as a result of divorce, nonmarital childbirth, parental military or occupational reasons, or parental incarceration. Chapter 7 turns to intergenerational relationships among adult children, parents, and grandparents. Peers, including adult siblings and friends, are covered in chapter 8.

Chapter 9 focuses exclusively on computer-mediated communication (CMC) and in doing so cuts across many relationship types, including relationships formed online and offline.

Chapter 10 returns to cultural assumptions, offers propositional conclusions, notes gaps in the extant literature, and outlines some practical implications. The closing chapter proposes extensions to one particular program of research on relational maintenance to be inclusive of the relationships considered herein.

A wide variety of research has been conducted on LDRs and cross-residential relationships; thus, no two chapters follow exactly the same format. However, within each chapter on a specific relational form, an attempt has been made to offer an approximate number of individuals or relationships that are long distance. Similarly, for each relational type, parameters for success are articulated. The little that is known about maintaining relationships is also included in each chapter.

It is hoped that this book might serve as a heuristic, prompting more critical thinking about the varied and complex forms of LDRs and cross-residential relationships, reconsideration of cultural assumptions relevant to communication and close relationships, and theoretical and pragmatic advances toward understanding the manner and desirability of relational maintenance.

2

Rationale, Definitions, and Assumptions

Though academia has largely ignored LDRs, popular culture is obsessed with them, especially those that are romantic. Interest also extends to numerous other types of LDRs. Long-distance friendships, noncustodial parents, and other kinships such as long-distance grandparent–grandchild relationships, young adult–parent relationships, and sibships are the subjects of this text. First, it is necessary to delineate why the study of LDRs is valuable, provide working definitions of LDRs, relational maintenance, and outline cultural assumptions surrounding such relationships.

WHY STUDY LDRS?

Popular interest in LDRs is due in part to the sheer number of individuals involved in one form or another. The occurrence of long-distance families is increasing as more women seek careers, join the military, or go to prison. Committed unions without marriage are becoming more prevalent; thus, the number of long-distance, nonmarital unions past the college years will likely grow as well. Periods of heightened military deployments or economic instability are also correlated with a rise of families whose members live apart from each other. Divorce and children born to single, noncohabiting parents also continues to contribute to children living away from one parent.

LDRs are not limited to romantic partners or parents and young children. More young adults attend college or live separately from a parent before marriage or in the absence of marriage than in previous years. The image of extended families residing together in the recent past is predominantly a myth, and most extended families still do not reside together. Thus, relationships among relatives such as grandparents and grandchildren or adult siblings are likely to be across residences, if not across communities. Moreover, given the mobility of society, we often make close friends in one locale that we leave behind geographically.

In short, in addition to relatively long-standing reasons for families and friends to live apart for substantial periods (e.g., military duty), numerous societal trends are converging that contribute to an increased proportion of the population that is involved in some type of personal relationship maintained across distance or residential boundaries. Thus, given the number and multiplicity of forms of LDRs, their study is timely.

The current popular fascination with LDRs has not been widely shared by scholars of communication or other social scientists. In 1995, Wood and Duck referred to LDRs as "understudied," and overall the scene has changed little since that time. However, it is not the ubiquitous nature and vacuous knowledge of LDRs alone that make the topic worthy of study. When these factors are considered in conjunction with U.S. cultural assumptions about the nature of close personal relationships and the communication considered necessary to maintain them, LDRs merit notice.

DEFINITIONS

Before turning to the assumptions surrounding relationships, it is first necessary to provide working definitions of relationships, LDRs, and relational maintenance.

Defining Relationships

Delineating the scope of *relationship* and *interaction* is a useful academic exercise challenging social scientific disciplines to engage in self-examination and refinement of theoretical positions. What constitutes a relationship, much less a close relationship, has been debated by numerous scholars, and that debate will not be resolved here. (See Duck, Acitelli, & Nicholson, 2000; Conville & Rogers, 1998, for insightful discussions of what defines a relationship and the implications attached to adopting various definitions of relationships.)

For some, LDRs are an inherent oxymoron; relationships are conceived as existing only when participants are interacting in the same physical space or are otherwise interacting in some manner, such as through mediated means. Relationships are bound by interaction (Goffman, 1983; Rogers, 1998).

Others take a cognitive approach, contending that relationships go beyond copresence; social relationships do not cease simply because members are not in physical presence or engaging in interaction (Sigman, 1991). It is acknowledged that such a perspective is not endorsed in most relational communication scholarship (Sigman, 1991). However, scholars must examine how relation- ships extend beyond any specific transaction (Sigman, 1998). Though the study of interaction is important, "there is a danger in research that limits relationships to interaction or treats relationship and interaction as largely synonymous" (Sigman, 1991, p. 108). For most of us moving throughout our daily lives, such distinctions carry little import. The position taken here is that relationships are both based in mutual interactions and go beyond interactions. Though "our relationships are derived from previous communicative exchanges, it is our mental images of them that creates their reality for us" (Wilmot, 1995, p. 3). In other words, relationships are continued in our minds; individual-level constructions are present in every relationship (Kenny, 1988). One's affective feelings for or perception of a relationship with one's spouse does not cease to exist simply because interaction is not occurring at a given moment. Communication, relationships, and perceptions are the same phenomenon; they are simply viewed from different vantage points (Sillars, 1998).

Obviously, carried to the extreme, completely cognitive relationships that are formed outside of mutual interaction might range from mild parasocial relationships[1] to delusional encounters with imaginary friends named Fred. Yet, debating the line among delusion, parasocial relationships, and true relationships is not ventured here. For example, if a grandfather gains comfort through a mental construction of a relationship with a grandchild he has never met, far be it from a scholar to declare that the grandfather has no relationship with his grandchild.

In fact, society deems that the grandparent does have a relationship, of some kind, with the grandchild by virtue of the fact that they are related legally or biologically, or both. They are culturally considered grandparent and grandchild. In other words, relationships exist and are maintained not only in our minds, but also through culturally recognized structures and conventions. Relationships are conferred on individuals, whether they like it or not. For example, another grandparent may disavow a grandchild; nonetheless, the relationship exists because of its ascribed status. In short, subjective perceptions of the mere existence of a relationship may be out of step of with interactional parameters or societal relational definitions.

Following Sigman (1991), Rawlins (1994) offered a scheme for classifying friendships, which is extended here as applicable to many other types of relationships. Rawlins considered friendships as active, dormant, or commemora-

---

[1]Parasocial relationships are those in which an individual feels an affinity for a media personality, sometimes mentally participating in the lives of this personality (see Giles, 2002).

tive. Active relationships are characterized by "availability, satisfactory contact, and emotional commitment" (p. 292). Dormant (or latent) relationships "share a valued history and/or maintain sufficient contact to anticipate or remain eligible for resumption of the friendship at any time" (p. 292). Other relationships are commemorative. These remain meaningful "as poignant symbols of particular places and moment of the life course" (p. 292). Rawlins's descriptions offer a useful way to consider multiple forms of relationships and thus are used throughout this text.

Defining LDRs

LDRs defy precise definitions. They may best be considered as an injunctive construct. Injunctive concepts do not have sharp lines of demarcation but rather gradually merge into neighboring concepts (Lorenz, 1966). Instead of attempting a formal definition of this fuzzy set of relationships, a guiding principle is adopted: Relationships are considered to be long distance when communication opportunities are restricted (in the view of the individuals involved) because of geographic parameters and the individuals within the relationship have expectations of a continued close connection. In this view, cross-residential relationships, such as those between parents and nonresidential children, may be considered a form of an LDR, even if the physical residences are geographically close. The term LDR here should be read to be inclusive of cross-residential relationships.

Defining Relational Maintenance

Maintenance is both a state and a process (Duck, 1994a; Stafford, 1994). As a state it has a temporal form. "Most scholars do agree about when maintenance occurs—namely, just after a relationship has finished beginning and just before it has started to end" (Montgomery, 1993, p. 205; see also Dindia, 1994; Duck, 1994a).

However, viewing maintenance as a "middle" period is remiss when applied to many forms of relationships other than those that are romantic. Similarly, neither relational development nor demise is particularly meaningful for some relationships, such as nonvoluntary, culturally ascribed kinships (see Hess, 2003). Also, some relationships may develop, and instead of dissolving, be redefined, such as when ex-spouses reconfigure their relationship from one as a romantically involved couple who also coparent to one based solely on coparenting.

Maintenance is also a process, and in moving to this level more conceptual tangles transpire. Multiple definitions of relational maintenance as a process have been offered (see Dindia & Canary, 1993). The definition adopted here is the one offered by Stafford and Canary (1991): Maintenance behaviors serve to sustain "the nature of the relationship to the actor's satisfaction" (p. 220). This comports with a process definition of maintenance as serving to keep a relationship in a specific condition or state (Dindia & Canary, 1993).

Communication processes of maintenance are of primary interest to scholars of communication, yet other mechanisms also serve to maintain relationships. As noted earlier, and will be revisited, relational maintenance may also occur through sociocultural presumptions of relationship status or mental constructions.

One purpose of this book is to synthesize the little that is known about maintaining LDRs. In most cases, success encompasses the continuance of the relationship, but not always; sometimes, defunct is the preferred relational state, though this is seldom societally recognized as a success (Masuda & Duck, 2002). One does not have to look far to uncover dysfunctional relationships that should be terminated, such as abusive relationships. As another example, in chapter 4 it is argued that the continuance of long-distance college dating relationships is not necessarily functional. In short, although mechanisms of relational maintenance are a focus of this text, no argument is made that the maintenance of any particular relationship is inherently better than its demise.

CULTURAL ASSUMPTIONS RELEVANT TO LDRS

Though not all cultural groups within a society share conceptions to the same extent, and certainly neither do any two relational partners, general societal assumptions influence individuals' expectations of their relationships as well as expectations of social networks (Reis & Knee, 1996). In other words, most people have significant social and cultural knowledge about what certain types of relationships should be like. This knowledge influences individual expectations or implicit theories and subsequent behavior as well as interpretations of behaviors (Koerner & Fitzpatrick, 2002).

LDRs are problematic for relational scholars as they persist in contradiction to many widely held U.S. cultural convictions about the nature of communication, proximity, and close relationships. Of course, not all separations contradict societal expectations and some do more so than others. Absences can be evaluated on the extent to which they violate social rules (Sigman, 1998). Yet, commonly held beliefs include:

1. Frequent FtF communication is necessary for close relational ties.
2. Geographic proximity is necessary for close relationships.

3. Family members, couples, and parents and young children are supposed to share a residence.
4. Shared meaning is necessary for close relationships.

Each of the aforementioned assumptions is explained in turn. They continue to be challenged in the following chapters as an understanding of LDRs is sought. In addition, assumptions unique to each relational form also are addressed in their respective chapters.

Assumption 1

Frequent FtF communication is necessary for close personal relationships. The predominant U.S. cultural presumption is that close relationships are characterized by frequent FtF contact and reciprocally, frequent FtF contact is necessary for close relationships. In U.S. society, FtF interaction is the preferred primary mode of communication in intimate relationships (O'Sullivan, 2000).

Conventional wisdom holds that this frequent FtF contact should include both in-depth disclosures and casual or small talk for relationships to thrive (Duck & Pittman, 1994; Parks, 1995). Concomitantly, infrequent contact, increases in distance, and increases in time between interactions have been seen as classic hallmarks of relational demise (Miller & Parks, 1982). Weak relationships are characterized by infrequent, limited interaction (Granovetter, 1983). Despite notions of relationships as mental constructions that exist beyond copresence (Berger & Kellner, 1964; Berger & Luckmann, 1966; Sigman, 1991; Wilmot, 1995), it is through daily talk that such mental creations of relationships are thought to occur and stabilize (Duck & Pittman, 1994). Satisfied couples engage in more conversation across a greater variety of topics than dissatisfied couples and spend time in the evening talking about their day (Richmond, 1995; Vangelisti & Banski, 1993). Individuals perceive daily talk with relational partners as an indication of the healthy continuation of their relationship (Duck, Rutt, Hurst, & Strejc, 1991).

Talk is not the only valued aspect of daily interaction. Simply spending time together is a commonly reported means of relational maintenance (Dainton & Stafford, 1993; Dindia & Baxter, 1987). In summarizing research, Vangelisti (2002) concluded that the amount of time romantic partners spend together on a day-to-day basis is a global indicator of relational satisfaction: "People who are happy with their relationships not only spend more time together, they engage in activities that make their time together particularly rewarding" (p. 660). In their review of the literature on marriage, Reissman, Aron, and Bergen (1993) reached a similar conclusion: The time couples spend engaging in leisure activities, such as talking or sharing tasks, is related to their relational satisfaction.

Such expectations are not confined to romantic relationships. FtF communication has been argued to be necessary to sustain family relationships (Vogl-Bauer, 2003). The entire family is also defined through interaction, though it is seldom studied as a whole. Burgess (1926) observed that any given family may be best thought of as a set of "interacting personalities" (p. 3). This view still holds: "A family's construction of social reality is represented in the family members' interactions" (Fitzpatrick & Caughlin, 2002, p. 745).

Parental time spent interacting daily with children is considered to be an indicator of child well-being by U.S. government offices (Fields, Smith, Bass, & Lugaila, 2001). Family scholars concur that routine frequent positive interactions between parents and children lay the foundation for numerous aspects of children's development (Satir, 1988). Though clearly all interaction between parents and children is not positive, frequency of contact is the most studied aspect of communication in relationships between nonresidential parents and children. By and large, the U.S. societal view is that even among divorced or never-married parents, children's overall adjustment is facilitated when they have frequent contact with both parents (Hetherington & Stanley-Hagan, 1997).

This is not to say that frequency of FtF contact is the only communication construct of relevance in close relationships, and as is demonstrated throughout this volume, nor is it necessarily even important. When investigations do move beyond frequency of FtF contact, they typically do not move far. Frequency of contact by any means is considered an indicator of the state of the relationship in numerous investigations. Sheer amount of contact is, however, the single most frequently examined construct in research on various forms of LDRs. Perhaps this is because the ambiguous construct of "frequent" FtF interaction is at the core of current cultural conceptualization of close relationships (O'Sullivan, 2000). The physical copresence required for FtF interaction is conspicuously absent in LDRs (Sahlstein, 2004). Thus, how, or even if, geographically separated individuals maintain close relational ties is immediately called into question.

Assumption 2

Geographic proximity is necessary for close relationships. Based on the first assumption, it is immediately obvious why proximity is considered necessary to sustain close relationships. Whether the relationship of interest is adult children and parents, children and grandparents, adult siblings, or friendships, most research takes as its focal point a presumption of an association between proximity and frequency of interaction and a presumption that frequency of interaction breeds positive relationships. The closer relational partners live to each other, the more opportunities for FtF interaction are possible. Strong ties have been viewed as those that are in near proximity and offer easy frequent access to provide companionship, social support, advice, and emotional assistance (Granovetter, 1983; Wellman, 1999). This inevitably leads to the question: What are close relationships?

General expectations for romantic partners, whether married or not, are based on companionship, love, and intimacy. Most college students consider friendship and passionate love as important aspects of their relationships (Sprecher & Regan, 1998). Societal expectations also include providing care, in terms of instrumental and emotional support, as well as affection in romantic relationships (Cutrona, 1996).

LDRs are in danger of failing to meet society's typical relational expectations. Referring to romantic relationships, Le and Agnew (2001) concluded, "It may be more difficult for partners to fulfill each other's relationship-related needs when separated by great geographic distance" and suggested that "one's relational partner needs to be physically accessible for need fulfillment" (p. 436). Disadvantages are assumed to be experienced in emotional, instrumental, and social realms by individuals in long-distance dating relationships and marriages (Groves & Horm-Wingerd, 1991).

Expectations for companionship and support extend to close familial relationships and close friendships. The family has shifted from an institution based on law and custom to one based on companionship and love (Burgess, Locke, & Thomes, 1971). Fitzpatrick and Caughlin (2002) endorsed Wamboldt and Reiss's (1989) view of a family, which prioritizes intimacy, interdependence, group identity, and a sense of history. This places a great emphasis on communication as the means through which such facets are achieved (Fitzpatrick & Caughlin, 2002).

U.S. society, in general, does not hold all of the same expectations for extended family members or adult nonromantic relationships, such as the adult child–parent relationships or friendships. Nonetheless, for relationships to be considered close, geographic proximity and frequent interaction are still often believed to be necessary. Proximity makes possible the accessibility considered foundational for relationships among all ages and generations (Lye, 1996).

Close friends are also supposed to live near each other to provide support and companionship. If friends do not live physically close, they have been thought to be inherently less emotionally close: "People who do not see each other frequently—for whatever reason— ...simply cannot be as close, other things being equal, as people who *do* spend a lot of time together" (Berscheid, Snyder, & Omoto, 1989, p. 794). In this view, friends who move to different locations must automatically become less emotionally connected.

The reader has undoubtedly noticed that an attempt to define a close relationship has been side-stepped. What constitutes closeness within similar relationships, much less what constitutes close relationships across various relational forms and co-cultures, is not uniformly agreed on. Nonetheless, this poorly conceived, seldom agreed on, variously operationalized, global construct of closeness in one form or another constitutes the core conceptualization of successful romantic, kin, and friend relationships in most relational research.

Assumption 3

"Family" is supposed to share a residence. The permeating presence of this assumption is discussed in regard to multiple family forms and dyadic family relationships.

Romantic Relationships and Young Child–Parent Relationships

In current U.S. society we accept or expect that friends, adult children, and adult siblings will live in different residences or different geographic locations, though we question how close or meaningful these distal relationships are. We do not expect romantic partners, whether dating, married, or otherwise committed, or nuclear families to live far apart. By definition, a nuclear family is one that shares a residence (Fitzpatrick & Caughlin, 2002).

One presumption is that dual-career couples who live apart for occupational reasons desire to live together at some point (Winfield, 1985), although one study found a small percentage of couples desired the commuting arrangement to be permanent (Farris, 1978). Research on romantic partners in the Netherlands revealed that many couples desire to continue separate residences indefinitely (Levin & Trost, 1999). The extent to which long-distance romantic partners desire to share residences eventually or prefer to live apart is in need of further investigation. Moreover, for many variations of LDRs, such as nonresidential parents and children, grandparents and grandchildren, and adult siblings or friends, shared residence is not an eventual goal.

In fact, since antiquity, a proportion of romantic partners and families have not resided together for significant periods. Even Homer's Penelope awaited the return of Odysseus when duty called him away to save Troy and rescue Helen. In select cultures and historical periods, husband and wife have not lived together, nor have parent and child; the communal Israeli Kibbutz serves as one example (Spiro, 1954). Noncohabitating marital relationships are not uncommon today in many cultures (see chap. 5, this volume), including the United States.

Nonetheless, coresidence is a component of virtually every standard sociological definition of marriage (Rindfuss & Stephen, 1990). Rindfuss and Stephen (1990) proffered that given the number of married individuals who

live apart for numerous reasons aside from consideration of divorce, cohabitation should not be assumed to be a defining characteristic of marriage but
rather a variable within marriage.

Families with young children are also expected to share the same residence.
The classic definition of a family as a "social group characterized by common
residence, economic cooperation, and reproduction" (Murdock, 1949, p. 1) has
stood as a standard for many years. This definition was reinforced by Parsons's
(1965) functional approach to families. As Gerstel and Gross (1984) pointed
out, Parsons assumes that a single shared residence is necessary for "the performance of family functions" (p. 199).

"In spite of the obvious problems, most family research still uses 'the household' as the working definition of the family" (Fitzpatrick & Caughlin, 2002, p.
727)—so does the U.S. government. The U.S. Census Bureau offers the following definition: "Family. A family is a group of two people or more (one of whom is
the householder) related by birth, marriage, or adoption and residing together"
(U.S. Census Bureau, 2002). Until recently, family textbooks have also continued to define the family in terms of a single residence, although of late the term
binuclear has been invoked to recognize children of divorced parents.

Scholars have recognized that families may span households, primarily because of divorce or nonmarital childbirth. However, if parents are married it is
assumed that a single residence is shared by all. Apparently, marital or family
noncohabitation is a concept many Americans find difficult to grasp. Unless
separated as a result of traditional occupational demands of the husband, such
as military duty or business travel, individuals in such relationships often encounter resistance or at least curiosity, if not suspicion, from their extended
families or social networks (Gerstel & Gross, 1984).

If children do not live with both parents, the mother is the culturally preferred primary caregiver. Thus, most research on nonresidential parents examines father absence. (The exception has been the recent upsurge in
research on the military mother; see chap. 5, this volume). The concept of
mother absence has generally been considered outlandish given the tender
years doctrine,[2] which privileges child and mother as the natural unit that is

---

[2]In early U.S. history in the case of divorce, common law and common practice recognized the father as custodian. In the landmark case Pennsylvania v. Addicks (1813), Chief Justice William
Tilghman awarded custody to the mother: "It appears to us that considering their (the two daugh-
ters') tender age, they stand in need of that kind of assistance, which can be afforded by none so well
as a mother" (Frost-Knappman & Cullen-Dupont, 1997). This case was significant in many ways:
First, the court took into account the children's best interests; second, common law precedence was
changed from the presumption of the father as custodian to mother; and third, the concept that the
mother and father cooperate in the father's visitation of the children is included. Tilghman declared
that the mother should not interfere with the father's right to see his children and she should accom-
modate his visits or allow the children to visit him, and he should not attempt to remove the children
to another geographic location. The "tender years" doctrine took root here and by the turn of the
century the presumption of the natural custodian had shifted from the father to the mother.

inherently best for the children. The tender years doctrine, although historically recent, has often preempted the separation of mothers and children whether through court or family decisions. Nonetheless, a significant number of mothers are separated from their children because of employment (military or civilian), divorce, or incarceration.

Extended Family Relationships

Thus far, the idea of family has focused on dyads or families with young children. However, families exist beyond this narrow view. "For many Americans, multigenerational bonds are becoming more important than nuclear family ties for well-being and support over the course of their lives" (Bengston, 2001, p. 3).

Family membership should not be tied to coresidence. Rather, a family is "a continuing interplay among intertwined lives within changing kinship structure" (Riley, 1983, p. 447, as cited in Bedford & Blieszner, 2000, p. 160). Self-definitions of families, rather than definitions based on biological, legal, or structural criteria, are needed. Such self-definitions are not contingent on shared residences. Coresidence cannot be a criterion for defining multigenerational families (Bedford & Blieszner, 2000). In this society, most older adults prefer to live independently from other family members, and this preference does not negate the desire for close relationships with family members. The view that these people with whom they do not reside are any less family than older adults who do reside with family members does not take into account the realities of individual's perceptions of their own families. Many older adults simply prefer "intimacy at a distance" (Gratton & Haber, 1993).

The limited definition of family, as construed by most, also neglects much of what families do with and for each other, simply because they are family, even across residential boundaries (Bedford & Blieszner, 2000). Examples include parents who provide economic aid to adult children, adult children's involvement in the lives of their elderly parents, grandparents' provision of support to grandchildren, and siblings' response in times of need.

Assumption 4

Shared meanings and understanding are necessary for close relationships. Culturally, an overemphasis is placed on shared meaning and understanding as relational necessities. As Parks (1982, 1995) noted, deep disclosure is advocated to create shared worldviews, and these shared worldviews are in turn necessary for meaningful relationships. Social groups, such as families, are supposed to exhibit "high congruence, high accuracy, and high agreement" (Koerner &

Fitzpatrick, 2004, p. 182). Individuals in close relationships should develop a "fusion" of meanings (VanderVoort & Duck, 2000).

Obviously, whether shared meanings or understanding are necessary for close relationships depends on what is meant by these terms. Vulcan mind melds notwithstanding, it is doubtful that any scholars believe exactly the same meaning of anything can exist in the minds of any two individuals. In general, understanding does correspond with relational closeness (Sillars, 1998). Similarly, perpetual misunderstandings and completely different realities would not be functional for individuals who must interact frequently; rampant chaos would result (Sillars, 1998).

However, benefits of some misunderstandings have come to light (Parks, 1995; Sillars, 1998). Benevolent misunderstandings can smooth many relational difficulties (Simpson, Ickes, & Blackstone, 1995). The position taken here is that limited shared realities and a lack of understanding, especially in terms of positively distorted perceptions, may be highly functional, at times. This position is revisited throughout this volume.

CONCLUSIONS

Though each relationship is unique in that each develops its own "miniculture" (Wilmot, 1995), these minicultures take place within a context of other networks. It is at the intersection of idiosyncratic relational definitions, individuals' social and familial connections, and society at large that relationships transpire. LDRs present difficulties as they exist in opposition to many social conceptions of relationships.

Most people have mental prototypes for relationships that are formed on the basis of cultural interactions (Koerner & Fitzpatrick, 2002) and relational schemata. Prototypes refer to individuals' conceptions of central attributes or traits of a specific construct, in this case a specific type of relationship. Similarly, relational schemata refer to the organization of information in memory about relationships, including beliefs and expectations about relationships (see Holmes, 2000). However, individuals in an LDR may find their relationship is not in alignment with their own or others' relational schemata. Or they may find that neither they nor their networks have a relational schema to draw on for the enactment of their form of LDR.

The position is taken that, regardless of scholarly debate as to what constitutes a relationship, individuals see their relationships as continuing when not physically in each other's company. If this premise is accepted, why does physical absence matter so much? It matters because physical proximity allows for the frequent FtF talk, companionship, shared leisure activities, and provision of support that are considered the basis of close relationships.

In general, in U.S. culture, close relational bonds of any type are conceived as contingent on interaction, companionship, and intimacy, all of which presume a rather high degree of FtF contact. The absence of this supposed fundamental condition is exactly what makes LDRs of particular interest to students of communication and close relationships: LDRs contravene culturally held beliefs about the role of communication in close personal relationships. A plurality of LDR forms survive and even thrive. These include numerous romantic, family, and friendship arrangements. LDRs, then, provide a natural condition in which to examine assumptions about communication, close relationships, and relational maintenance. It is to this end that the following chapters are presented.

3

Theoretical Orientations

Though multiple theoretical perspectives[3] have been applied to the study of relational maintenance, most research on LDRs has been atheoretical. Moreover, few relational maintenance paradigms have been applied to LDRs of any form. Given the ubiquitous nature of LDRs and the plethora of theories relevant to either relational maintenance, LDRs, or both, this chapter is presented with two primary goals in mind. The first is to review theoretical positions that have been invoked either directly or indirectly, or have considerable potential for the extension to LDRs. These overviews are provided to aid the reader, who might be unfamiliar with these approaches, in navigating the subsequent chapters. The second goal is to urge further theoretically grounded research on the maintenance of LDRs.

To achieve these objectives, four predominant perspectives to relational maintenance are considered. These are followed by four theories that have not been labeled as approaches to relational maintenance but have been applied to the study of LDRs or have been used to examine relational phenomenon especially relevant to LDRs. In many instances, placement of perspectives is somewhat arbitrary, as many approaches are informed by more than one theoretical orientation. A social cognitive perspective is then reviewed.

Because of space limitations and the number of readily available summaries of these theoretical orientations, explication here is minimal. Rather, the reader is pointed to one or more examples of the application of each theory in subsequent chapters and provided at least one suggestion for fur-

---

[3]It is recognized that the terms *theory, model, framework, perspective*, and the like are used indiscriminately and interchangeably here. Given the purposes here, metatheoretical debates as to differences among such constructs and what counts as a theory per se are beyond the scope of this book. The reader is referred to Ritzer (1992) and Fiske and Shweder (1986) and for discussions on metatheory and the philosophy of science.

ther reading. Theories primarily applied to computer-mediated LDRs are discussed in chapter 9.

THEORETICAL APPROACHES TO RELATIONAL MAINTENANCE

Duck (1988) has often been cited for his insightful observation that most of us spend more time maintaining relationships than we do developing or disengaging from them, yet relational maintenance had received little scholarly attention. A few years after making this observation, Duck (1994b) noted that although some progress had been made, relational maintenance remained a "vast unstudied void in relational research" (p. 45). This has changed considerably, as he now notes—that the study of relational maintenance is now regarded as central (Masuda & Duck, 2002).

Four approaches are put forth as having sustained theoretical programs of work on relational maintenance by Canary and Zelley (2000). Two emanate from social exchange theory and one from dialectical theory. The fourth is Gottman's (e.g., Gottman & Levenson, 2002) interactional approach. Duck's (e.g., 1988, 1994b) vision of relational maintenance as shared meaning is also explicated, as he has prompted the study of relational maintenance more than any other theoretician and his work informs the propositions offered in the final chapter of this text. These are by no means all of the orientations that have been taken to relational maintenance. For a broader range of perspectives and relational contexts, the reader is advised to see volumes edited by Canary and Dainton (2003), Canary and Stafford (1994a), and Harvey and Wenzel (2001, 2002).

Social Exchange Theories

According to social exchange theory, individuals form, develop, and terminate relationships based on the rewards and costs, or potential rewards and costs, associated with that relationship (Kelley & Thibaut, 1978). Rewards are sources of positive reinforcement such as social acceptance, instrumental services, power, or prestige. Costs are punishments or lost rewards such as investments of time and effort (Blau, 1964). Roloff (1981) provided an outstanding overview of social exchange approaches. Two variations of social exchange theory have been applied to relational maintenance in general, and to a lesser extent, to LDRs in particular: an equity-based approach and an investment model.

The perspective that has most directly applied equity to relational maintenance was first articulated by Stafford and Canary (1991; Canary & Stafford, 1992, 1994a, 2001). This position draws on equity theory as outlined by Adams (1965), Hatfield, Traupmann, Sprecher, Utne, and Hay (1985), Sprecher (1986), and Walster (Hatfield), Berscheid, and Walster (1973).

"Equity theory predicts that people are content when both persons have equal ratios of inputs to outcomes, that people are distressed when involved in an inequitable relationship and that people try to restore and maintain equity" (Canary & Stafford, 1994b, p. 7). Overbenefited individuals perceive that they get more out of a relationship than they put into it, whereas underbenefited individuals perceive that they get less out of a relationship than they put into it. Being either overbenefited or underbenefited should result in emotional distress; equitable relationships should be satisfying (Sprecher, 1986).

When a relationship is inequitable, and thus dissatisfying, individuals are motivated, in theory, to restore equity (Adams, 1965). Means to adjust equity include changing one's costs, changing one's rewards, cognitively distorting the inequity by altering the value of costs or rewards, exiting the relationship, persuading one's partner to change his or her efforts, altering one's bases for comparison, and punishing the partner (Canary & Stafford, 2001, derived from Adams, 1965; Walster (Hatfield), et al., 1973).

The identification of maintenance efforts enacted by relational partners, their association with desired features of relationships, and the influence of perceptions of equity on these behaviors has been the foremost quest of this program or work. An instrument to assess five global behaviors was developed by Stafford and Canary (1991; Canary & Stafford, 1992). These five behaviors are the most often studied and include positivity, assurances, openness, networks, and tasks. Additional studies have identified various behaviors in several relational types, though there seems to be more overlap than difference. (See Table 3.1 for a list of maintenance behaviors identified in this program of work, and see Stafford, 2003, for a detailed explanation of these behaviors and a summary of this research program). This approach is revisited and elaborated in chapter 11 wherein propositions are offered to explicitly extend this work to the study of LDRs. Oswald and Clark's (2003) exploration of the costs and rewards of long-distance friendships most clearly illustrates the extension of this theory to LDRs (see chap. 8, this volume).

The second variation of a social exchange approach is Rusbult's (1980, 1983; Rusbult, Drigotas, & Verette, 1994) investment model derived from Kelley and Thibaut's (1978) concept of interdependence. Relationships are considered satisfying when they are perceived as rewarding on a comparative basis. Comparisons are made against one's expectations based on previous relational experiences and one's perceptions of potential alternatives. Commitment is central to this approach as it influences relational maintenance behaviors. An important contribution of this model is the explicit recognition of both psychological and communicative processes as relational maintenance mechanisms. In the investment model, maintenance is influenced by commitment. Also, one's level of investment drives cognitive distortions. If investments are high, potential alternatives are viewed derogatorily and present relationships are distorted positively. Rusbult's investment model seems espe-

TABLE 3.1

Relational Maintenance Behaviors Identified by Stafford, Canary, and Colleagues

Behavior	Examples
Positivity[a]	Try to act nice and cheerful. Attempt to make our interactions enjoyable.
Openness[a]	Encourage him or her to disclose thoughts and feelings to me.
Assurances[a]	Stress my commitment to him or her. Imply that our relationship has a future.
Social network[a]	Like to spend time with our same friends. Focus on common friends and affiliations.
Sharing tasks[a]	Help equally with tasks that need to be done. Do my fair share of the work we have to do.
Conflict management[b]	Apologize when I am wrong. Cooperate in how I handle disagreements.
Advice[b]	Give him or her my opinion on things going on in his or her life.
Focus on self	Work on a degree. Focus on spiritual or religious development. Make sure I look good.
Joint activities	Spend time hanging out. Visit my brother when he is away at school.
Mediated communication	Write letters.Use e-mail to keep in touch. Communicate on the phone.
Avoidance/antisocial behaviors	Am not completely honest with him/her. Avoid or act badly so he or she doesn't want to get closerc to me.
Humor	Call him or her by a funny nickname.
No flirting[c]	Avoid flirting with him or her. Do not allow myself to be in a romantic place with him or her. Do not encourage overly familiar behavior.
Support[c]	Comfort him or her in time of need.
Share activity[c]	Share special rituals with him or her. Share specific routine activities with him or her.
Religion	Attend church together.Pray about our marriage.
Small talk	Talk about our day.Talk about little things.
Affection	Displays of fondness. Kiss each other good-bye in the morning.

Gay/ lesbian supportive	Live in supportive settings.environments
Be in nonjudgmental settings.	

Note. Table abbreviated from Stafford (2003) as adapted and extended from Canary and Stafford (2001). Examples adapted from Canary and Stafford (1992), Canary, Stafford, Hause, and Wallace (1993), Dainton and Stafford (1993), Diggs and Stafford (1998), Haas and Stafford (1998), Messman, Canary, and Hause (2000), and Stafford, Dainton, and Haas (2000).

Categories are those directly from work with Stafford or Canary as an author or coauthor. Items without a superscript have not yet been developed into measurements.

[a]The five original factors from Stafford and Canary (1991).

[b]Additional factors from Stafford et al. (2000).

[c]Additional factors from Messman et al. (2000).

cially well suited for the examination of long-distance romantic relationships; however, it has seldom been applied to this population. An exception (see chap. 4, this volume) is the examination of moral commitment in college dating LDRs (Lydon, Pierce, & O'Regan, 1997). For a summary of this program of research see Rusbult, Olsen, Davis, and Hannon (2001).

Dialectical Perspectives

An emphasis on change and contradictory forces forms the basis of dialectical perspectives. Relationships experience simultaneous pushes and pulls in differing directions. These tensions occur internally within a dyad, between relational partners, and externally, between the partners as a unit and others. Frequently noted pairs of dialectical tensions include autonomy and connection, stability and change, and openness and closedness. Sahlstein (2004) applies a dialectical approach to long-distance dating relationships (see chap. 4, this volume).

Dialectical approaches to relational maintenance focus on managing or negotiating these inherent oppositional forces (Montgomery, 1993). These tensions are in a constant state of dynamic flux and cannot be resolved; rather, they are managed. Several means of coping with these forces have been suggested such as alternating from one extreme to the other or attempting to ignore the tension. The most effective way of managing these has been argued to be through a perceptual cognitive shift or reframing the tension, so that it is not seen as such. (For a complete discussion of relational dialectics, see Baxter & Montgomery, 1996.)

A Behavioral Approach

Gottman's work is included here as it as been at the forefront in the prediction of long-term relationship stability and offers incredible potential for application to long-distance romantic relationships. However, to this author's knowledge, as this approach has not been researched directly in conjunction with LDRs, the reader is not pointed to an example of this work in upcoming chapters.

Gottman (e.g., Gottman, 1979, 1994; Gottman, Coan, Carrere, & Swanson, 1998; Gottman & Levenson, 2002) has extensively examined the relationships among specific communicative sequences, physiological arousal, and relational stability. He also emphasized the perceptual screen though which these interactions are interpreted. This view follows from attribution theory (Heider, 1958), wherein interpretations of a partner's behaviors as positive or negative is highly contingent on stable internal views of partner's traits. If a partner comes to view the other, overall, positively or negatively, messages tend to be interpreted in correspondence with that general view (Hawkins, Carrere, & Gottman, 2002). In short, as much, if not more, importance is placed on nurturing positive visions of relational partners as on communication behaviors themselves, as positive perceptions of partners influence the interpretation of interaction in a cascading manner, a process Gottman (1994) refers to as positive sentiment override.

Meaning as Relational Maintenance

Duck has prompted the study of relational maintenance more than any other scholar. His (e.g., see Duck, 1988, 1994a, 1994b; Masuda & Duck, 2002) vision is that relationships are maintained through everyday talk, as it is routine ordinary talk that forms the basis of relational realities. This position has its roots in social constructionist views, which in turn may be traced to symbolic interactionism.

Symbolic interactionism was formulated by Mead (1934) and advanced by his student, Blumer (1969), who coined the term *symbolic interactionism*. At its most basic level, symbolic interaction is concerned with the problem of how meaning is constructed. Meaning is derived from the interpretation of symbols by individuals and social groups engaged in social interaction.

Symbolic interactionism is a broad perspective from which many theories are derived, including dramatism (e.g., Goffman, 1959, 1983), role theory (e.g., Kantor & Lehr, 1975), and the genre of social constructionist perspectives (e.g., Berger & Luckmann, 1966), wherein relational realities are jointly constructed by relational participants. Rules, roles, norms, and meanings for and about interaction are developed through interaction and, in turn, shape interaction.

One specific example of the dramaturgical perspective of self-fulfilling prophecies and manipulation of self-presentation (Goffman, 1959) is seen in computer mediated relationships (see chap. 9, this volume). Social constructionism can be seen in the examination of roles in nonresidential fathers' relationships with their children (see chap. 10, this volume). Charon (2004) provided a thorough introduction to symbolic interactionism, and Leeds-Hurwitz (1995) offered a discussion of social constructionist views in general.

Returning to Duck (e.g., Duck, 1988, 1994a, 1994b; Duck et al., 1991; Masuda & Duck, 2002), maintenance refers to keeping a relationship "running well." Anything people to do sustain their relationships is inherently a maintenance skill; it is making sense of relationships that ultimately allows their continuation (Masuda & Duck, 2000). Routinely, seemingly trivial, everyday talk is essential. Talk "continues to embody partners' understanding or shared meanings, and it continues to represent their relationship to one another in ways that each accepts and is comfortable with, or which 'ratify' the relationship (Duck, 1994b, p. 54). This approach is included here precisely because of its emphasis on routine talk. Thus, how LDRs are maintained in accordance with this perspective is an intriguing problem to be considered. This perspective is revisited in chapter 11, this volume.

Summary

All of these orientations to relational maintenance involve both behavioral and cognitive processes, though the relative emphasis varies. As is demonstrated in upcoming chapters, cognitions play a unique role in LDRs; thus each of these orientations has great potential for the study of LDRs. As a whole, however, an overarching limitation of these perspectives is the limited consideration of both nonromantic relationships and LDRs.

Four additional theories that have examined LDRs, either directly or indirectly, but that have not been deemed as relational maintenance approaches per se are now considered. This is not an exhaustive list of orientations with potential application to LDRs; rather, they are the theories most frequently invoked in the research informing the following chapters.

THEORIES RELEVANT TO LDRS

Attachment Theory

Attachment theory is often thought of as a mechanism for understanding caregiver–infant bonds (Ainsworth, Blehar, Waters, & Wall, 1978; Bowlby, 1973), though from its inception attachment was thought to operate through the life span. Attachment refers to "any form of behavior that results in a person attaining or retaining proximity to some other differentiated and preferred individual, usually conceived as stronger and/or wiser" (Bowlby, 1973, p. 185).

A life-span approach to attachment theory contends that adult children continue attachments with parents throughout their adulthood as do siblings (Cicirelli, 1995). Intriguingly relevant to LDRs is the proposed capacity for adults to sustain relationships through adulthood in absence of physical proximity through symbolic attachment. Long-distance marriages have been considered in light of attachment theory by Vormbrock (1993; see also chap. 5, this volume). The reader is referred to Cassidy and Shaver (2002) for a comprehensive volume on attachment theory.

Family Solidarity Theory

This sociological theory is concerned with family cohesion, especially affection, social support, and a sense of family history or identity across generations (e.g., Bengston, 2001; Bengston & Roberts, 1991).

One particularly germane aspect of family solidarity theory is the intergenerational stake hypothesis (Giarrusso, Stallings, & Bengston, 1995). Children report less close connections with older generations than vice versa. Children desire to achieve independence, whereas older generations desire generativity and thus offer more investments. This is purported to operate across the life span, though as individuals age the relationships become more reciprocal perhaps because of increased interdependence.

The negotiation of roles among the generations, such as the balance of cohesion and independence of young adults and their parents, is also a point of interest. Family solidarity theory is considered in the obligatory nature of sibling relationships (Bengston, 2001; see also chap. 8, this volume) and distal grandparent–grandchildren relationships by Harwood (2000b; see also chap. 7, this volume).

Family Life Span

This approach takes a cyclical developmental view of the individual and the family. The various stages or phases through which the individual within the family, as well as family phases, are considered. For example, a child moves through infancy, childhood, adolescence, and young adulthood. The family might move though stages such as newly married or the empty nest.

Within family life-span or development perspectives, interest is often on specific events. Event perspectives examine how specific transitions in the lives of family members affects their interaction. Though all families and individuals are considered to continue to develop across the life span, this approach generally does not adhere to universals; rather, the nature of change is embedded in a social and cultural environment. Chapter 8 includes a discussion of how events such as marriage, divorce, or the death of parents influence interaction patterns among siblings. See Carter and McGoldrick (1999) for an interesting compilation of works in this domain, including discussions of cultural implications.

Systems Theories

Systems perspectives are broad; many variations of systems theory exist even within the realm of close relationships. Examples include Bronfenbrenner's (1979) ecological system theory, Hinde's relationship perspective (Hinde & Stevenson-Hinde, 1987), and the Palo Alto's pragmatic perspective (Watzlawick, Beavin, & Jackson, 1967). Though these theories diverge in some crucial ways, they also converge in regard to critical components such as interdependence, wholeness, boundaries, homeostasis, and change (Stafford & Bayer, 1993).

Interdependence is the defining characteristic of systems (Stafford & Bayer, 1993). Interdependence within a systems view means everything one person does affects all others in the system. Systemic wholeness simply implies that the entire system must be considered; individuals or individual dyads cannot be understood apart from the larger system. Boundaries are structural properties that delineate subsystems; for example, a sibling group is a subsystem within the family system. Systems resist change; they strive to maintain the status quo (homeostasis). Yet change in systems is inevitable, albeit stressful.

Systems theories implicitly guide much of the study of LDRs, though they are seldom directly acknowledged. Potential points of application to LDRs include boundaries between children and the at-home parent, the tendency toward homeostasis of family members on the return of a previously absent member (see chap. 5, this volume), the reverberations through the family caused by the young adults departure from the parental home (see chap. 8, this volume), and the interface between long-distance families and friends or community, to name only a few. For a discussion of general systems theories, see Bahg (1990). Bochner and Eisenberg (1987) offer an overview of family systems theories.

SOCIAL COGNITION

On a fundamental level, social cognitive approaches to relationships entail both the role of interaction and mental processes in relational construction, maintenance, and demise. Social cognitive approaches to communication can be "subdivided into two nonexclusive categories: understanding the interrelationships of social cognition and social behavior and understanding the formation and organization of social cognition" (Knapp, Daly, Albada, & Miller, 2002, p. 15). In other words, some place more emphasis on the reciprocal nature of thought and communicative behavior; others place more emphasis on how individuals perceive and organize information. Both of these domains are relevant to LDRs.

Many of the aforementioned perspectives are either congruent with or informed by social cognitive approaches. For example, symbolic attachment, (1994b) emphasis on shared meaning, and all social constructionist orientations are, at least in part, in concert with social cognitive approaches to communication and relationships. Even equity theory allows for cognitive distortion in order to restore perceived equity (Adams, 1965). (See Honeycutt & Cantrill, 2001, for an interesting examination of the conjoint role of cognition and communication in romantic relationships.)

A particularly intriguing and apparently pervasive mental mechanism operating in LDRs is idealization. Globally, idealization refers to generalized positive bias toward one's partner or relationships (Schulman, 1974). Idealization has been operationalized as this global phenomenon; as illusions wherein individuals see their partners in a better light than partners see themselves (Murray, Holmes, & Griffen, 1996); as perceived relational superiority, wherein one views one's own relationships with more favor and optimism than other's relationships (Rusbult, Van Lange, Wildschut, Yovetich, & Verette, 2000; Taylor & Brown, 1988); or even as part and parcel of romantic love (Lindholm, 1998; Sternberg & Barnes, 1985).

Idealized images may arise through restricted communication (Schulman, 1974) and serve both positive and negative functions in relationships. In chapters 4 and 9 of this volume, concerns are raised about the risks of idealization in the formation of inaccurate or unrealistic and potentially unobtainable expectations in dating LDRs and computer-mediated LDRs, respectively, whereas in chapters 7 and 8 of this volume, probable benefits of idealized views of long-distance friends and relatives are touted.

CONCLUSIONS

The number of theoretical frameworks explicitly invoked in the study of LDRs is limited; the number of theories from various disciplines that inform some aspect of LDRs is seemingly infinite and only a select few have been mentioned here.

Many promising candidates beyond those previously enumerated warrant consideration and those listed could be applied much more fruitfully. Yet, the purpose here is not to outline programs of study but to point out that theoretically driven research devoted to LDRs is lacking, despite readily applicable theoretical foundations. Moreover, relational scholars and LDR participants have the potential for a unique symbiotic relationship: Given the theoretical and cultural primacy accorded communication for mere continuance of relationships, much less maintaining close affectional ones, LDRs are a natural laboratory in which to test numerous theories of relationships and communication. In addition, the opportunity to develop theoretically driven practical applications should be obvious. Some such applications are discussed in chapter ten, this volume.

4

Long-Distance
Dating Relationships

Long-distance dating relationships (LDDRs) among college students have garnered more research attention from scholars of interpersonal communication than any other single type of LDR (Aylor, 2003). Estimates indicate that anywhere from 25% to 50% of college students are involved in a long-distance dating relationship at any given time and 75% of college students have at some time been involved in at least one LDDR (Dellmann-Jenkins, Bernard-Paolucci, & Rushing, 1994; Guldner & Swensen, 1995). LDDRs may be as prevalent on college campuses as geographically close dating relationships (Stafford, Merolla, & Castle, 2004). Given the epidemic proportion of college students involved in LDDRs, attention is not unwarranted, although it is unfortunate that our knowledge of LDDRs comes solely from couples wherein at least one of the partners is a college student.

The exact definition of a long-distance dating relationship varies from report to report and even from individual to individual. Physical parameters such as mileage or living in different cites are sometimes used (e.g., Carpenter & Knox, 1986; Helgeson, 1994). Others have defined LDDRs as those that participants consider long-distance (Dellmann-Jenkins et al., 1994). Such a definition likely captures each individual's relational reality better than researcher-imposed constructions as even two members of the same couple have been found to disagree as to whether or not their relationship is, or ever has been, a long-distance one (Stafford et al., 2004).

SUCCESS

What people want to know most about romantic long-distance relationships is "Do they work?" Guldner considers long-distance romantic relationships as working if the couple remains intact. Apparently so do most scholars, counselors, and romantic partners. However, it is safe to assume that the desire is not only to remain intact, but also, consistent with the definition of maintenance offered in the first chapter of this volume, long-distance dating partners also want their relationships to be characterized by relational qualities such as satisfaction, liking, commitment, trust, and so on. In addition, LDDRs are generally presumed to be stressful and depressing for the individuals involved. Seemingly then, successful LDDRs are those that remain intact for an unspecified period of time, are characterized by positive relational features such as satisfaction, and the individuals involved in the relationship have an absence of stress or depression. These alleged markers of success are discussed next, first turning to distress and dysfunction.

Distress, Dysfunction, and Coping

Alarm over anguish ridden, forlorn college students wandering the halls of academia appears unwarranted, or at least unverified. The assumption that LDDRs are depressing or stressful might be traced to Wendel (1975). He was interested in the feelings of high school sweethearts when one or both went away to college. He concluded that students felt a sense of "separateness and distance" (p. 45).

The legacy of dysfunction, distress, and depression among individuals in LDDRs became entrenched with the findings of Westefeld and Liddell (1982). As college counselors, they reported being confronted by students in "angst" over their long-distance romances. Based on discussion forums with students who were having difficulty coping with their LDDRs, they enumerated several problematic areas including economic difficulty from telephone and travel expenses, ambiguity in defining the parameters of other geographically close relationships, determining the best use of their time when they were physically together, coping with roller-coaster like emotions, and assessing whether they should continue their relationships. The most often cited aspect of their work is the reported angst and emotional stress. Most overlooked is their insight that individuals in LDDRs have difficulty "evaluating the relationship while at a distance" (Westefeld & Liddell, 1982, p. 550). This oversight is addressed later in this chapter.

In response to the concerns raised by long-distance dating partners, Westefeld and Liddell (1982) conducted workshops as a forum for students to exchange advice and they summarized the students' recommendations. Suggestions included simply recognizing and accepting that the situation is stressful; developing support networks in their present community; developing "creative ways of communicating while at a distance" (p. 550); setting rules for the separation in advance while being aware these might need to be flexible; using their limited time together wisely; and being honest and open with each other. Focusing on the positive aspects of the separation and attempting to be optimistic about the relationship were also advised. Although often repeated as coping strategies (e.g., Aylor, 2003; Rohfling, 1995), these suggestions are yet to be confirmed as actually beneficial.

Insightfully, Westefeld and Liddell (1982) felt that the primary benefit of the workshops was simply the venue itself. The forums allowed students to form connections with and receive support from proximal individuals with similar circumstances. Research supporting the importance of developing proximal community ties for the provision of companionship, support, and the like remains consistent (e.g., Carpenter & Knox, 1986; Holt & Stone, 1988; Schwebel, Dunn, Moss, & Renner, 1992; Wilmot & Carbaugh, 1986). Thus, it is possible that these connections eased the separation for some individuals.

Westefeld and Liddell (1982) drew their conclusions about LDDRs based only on individuals who sought counseling. Holt and Stone (1988) found that the less satisfied students were with their long-distance relationships, the more likely they were to seek counseling. Thus, Westefeld and Liddell's conclusions (1982) may not be representative of most students in LDDRs.

Still, the proclamation that distance and distress go hand in hand continues to be propagated. Guldner (1996) based in an attachment paradigm (see chap. 2, this volume) claimed that separation from a romantic partner inherently results in distress. Although, he did find that students involved in LDRs reported "feeling blue" more often than students in proximal relationships, he reported major depression to be no more frequent among individuals in LDDRs than among those in geographically proximal relationships. Nor did he find any differences in distress or psychological functioning between individuals in LDDRs and geographically close ones. Similarly, although Le and Agnew (2001) found geographically close dating partners were better able to meet needs for companionship, sexual activity, security, and emotional involvement than long distance partners, this was not associated with negative emotions.

LDDRs simply do not seem to be as inherently or uniformly problematic as some have claimed (e.g. Guldner, 1996). For example, Knox, Zusman, Daniels, and Brantley (2002) reported that by 5 months of separation approximately 20% of LDDRs had ended and another 20% reported their relationships were worse. Alternatively, nearly 20% also indicated the separation made their relationship better and just more than 30% gave mixed responses. In addition, students in LDDRs perform better academically than those in geographically close relationships; they also are better rested (Guldner, 1992, 1996; Guldner & Swensen, 1995).

Other work has also found both benefits and drawbacks to LDDRs (Sahlstein, 2004; Stafford et al., 2004). Individuals appear to appreciate the separation in order to focus on school or career when apart and then focus on their relationships when together (Stafford et al., 2004). This type of segmentation also occurs in long-distance dual career couples (see chap. 5, this volume). Many individuals also like the freedom and autonomy of a LDDR and concurrently miss their partners and wish they could spend more time together (Stafford et al., 2004). Sahlstein (2004), working from a dialectical perspective (see chap. 2, this volume) revealed paradoxical contradictions in LDDRs. When the long-distance partners see each other in person, they report a sense of rejuvenation, a reduction in uncertainty about their relationships, and form memories to help sustain them when apart. They also report pressure to make sure their time spent together is high quality and avoid disagreements. When separated again, many express feeling let down or sad on returning to their everyday lives without their partners. Yet they simultaneously enjoy the anticipation of seeing each other when they are apart. Although the sample size is relatively small (20 couples), Sahlstein's (2004) in-depth interviews provide a picture of the complexities of LDDRs. Moreover, the themes she identified reiterate those revealed in research long-distance marriages (see Gerstel & Gross, 1984; Winfield, 1985).

Maintenance as Success

Research has often focused on success as stability of dating partners (Cate, Levin, & Richmond, 2002). Remaining a couple is unequivocally viewed as successful and desirable. For example, Schwebel et al. (1992) stated a goal of their study of LDDRs was to understand the factors "involved in preserving the relationships" (1992, p. 22) in order to aid college counselors in advising students.

By the criteria of remaining a couple, LDDRs are as successful if not more so than proximal couples. Stephen (1986) found that LDDRs were more stable across time than geographically close couples. Reske and Stafford (1989) found that, after 6 months, 30% of geographically close relationships and dissolved, but none of the LDDRs in their sample had. Stafford and Reske (1990) also found a pattern of greater stability among LDRRs. The same pattern was not replicated by VanHorn et al. (1997). However, the timeframe for the Van Horn et al. (1997) study was 11 to 12 weeks compared to 6 months, 9 months, and 2 years for the studies of Reske and Stafford (1989), Stafford and Reske (1990), and Stephen (1986), respectively, which may account for the differences in relational termination rates.

If we go beyond stability and include other relational features as success, LDDRs appear to fare quite well. Most studies have found equal or even higher levels of satisfaction, commitment, and trust in LDDRs compared to geographically close ones (Guldner & Swensen, 1995; Lydon, Pierce, & O'Regan, 1997; Schwebel, Dunn, Moss, & Renner, 1992; Stafford & Reske, 1990; Stephen, 1986; VanHorn, et al., 1997).

MAINTAINING LDDRS

Approval of one's romantic involvements by one's friendship network repeatedly has been found to play a role in the stability of dating relationships in general (Cate, Levin, & Richmond, 2002; Felmlee, 2001; Sprecher & Felmlee, 2000). Given that LDDRs violate norms of proximity, individuals are not always validated by nearby friends or families. Sahlstein (2004) reported that long-distance dating partners find that their immediate social networks play both a positive and a negative role in the maintenance of their long-distance relationships. College students in LDDRs are surrounded by others in similar situations with whom to commiserate. "Perhaps the unique college environment inoculates these relationships against the impact of deficits in time spent together" (Guldner & Swensen, 1995, p. 319).

Some research has found an association between frequency of face-to-face (FtF) interaction and relational success. Holt and Stone (1988) reported that college partners who physically saw each other less than once a month and lived under 250 miles apart were less satisfied than dating partners who saw each other more frequently. Similarly, Dainton and Aylor (2002) asked how often college LDDR individuals saw each other and found that those who answered "never" were less satisfied and less committed than individuals with "periodic face to face contact" (p. 127). They found FtF contact to be positively associated with satisfaction, trust, commitment, and lowered jealousy. However, their findings were not longitudinal.

In addition to FtF communication, LDDRs use a variety of mediated means. Couples who exchange letters are more likely to stay together than those who do not (Guldner, 1992, as cited in Guldner, 1996). Similarly, Stafford and Reske (1990) found letters to be more highly associated with feelings of satisfaction, love, satisfaction with communication, and idealization in the relationship than FtF or telephone contact. Dainton and Aylor (2002) found that telephone time and Internet use among dating partners were positively associated with relational success as defined by increased satisfaction, trust, commitment, and lowered jealousy. They did not find the same associations for letters. This may be a function of expectations and availability. Access to e-mail was greater on college campuses at the time of the Dainton and Aylor study than when the Stafford and Reske study was conducted. In fact, Stafford and Reske did not even ask about e-mail usage. (See chap 5, this volume, on the use of letters and e-mail among deployed military personal and their families, and chap 9, this volume, for more on the role of the Internet in LDRs).

Yet even with these mediated means, some FtF contact is still thought to be important. Dainton and Aylor (2002) found that long-distance partners with no FtF contact were less certain of their relationships and less trusting of their partners than those with some FtT contact.

If some level of FtF interaction is important, then how long is too long to go without physically being in each other's presence? Too long is perceived as just slightly longer than the partners usually go without seeing each other. Individuals who reported seeing each other every week felt that more than a week was too long. If seeing each other once a month was normative for a couple, then anything over once a month was felt to be too long (Stafford, 2004).

IDEALIZATION AS RELATIONAL MAINTENANCE

In contrast to U.S. cultural expectations about frequent FtF interaction as the cornerstone for close relationships, Guldner and Swensen (1995) concluded that the amount of time long-distance couples spent together played little role in the maintenance of the relationship. Moreover, Stafford and Reske (1990) found that the greater the proportion of interaction spent FtF compared to frequency of other modes, the less satisfied with the relationship, the less satisfied with the communication, and the more likely the demise of the dating relationship.

This seeming paradox of limited FtF interaction contributing to stability was noted by Stephen (1986). He surmised that geographically close couples have the luxury of virtually unlimited conversation about a vast array of topics; LDR participants, on the other hand, talk about a much more limited range of topics, such as issues "related to love and intimacy" (Stephen, 1986, p. 206). He proposes that individuals minimize the importance of talk for the maintenance of their relationships as well as depend more on the talk they do have to construct relational realities. Likewise, Guldner and Swenson (1995) concluded that talk or quantity of time together simply are "not central to relationship satisfaction, intimacy, trust, or commitment" but rather, "some other factor associated with even small amounts of time spent together" (p. 320) must sustain these relationships.

Idealization, as defined in chapter 2 of this volume, is proposed to be this mechanism. Restricted communication facilitates idealized images (Schulman, 1974; Stafford & Reske, 1990) and by default, LDDRs have restricted FtF communication. Stafford and Reske (1990) proposed that such positive illusions accounted for the longevity of geographically separated dating relationship; a lack of communication preempts couples from discovering undesirable attributes. Dainton and Aylor (2002) repeated this concern with idealization. They speculated that perhaps even long-distance couples with frequent, short, face-to-face visits may be acting on their "best behavior" allowing idealization to continue instead of actually becoming better acquainted. Other reports also suggest that LDDRs partners tend to present overly positive images of themselves to their partners when FtF (Sahlstein, 2004, Stafford et al., 2004). Long-distance partners avoid negative interactions when together to avoid ruining this precious time (Sahlstein, 2004; Stafford et al., 2004). When apart, they focus on plans for when together, ruminate about positive relational memories (Sahlstein, 2004), and day-dream about their partners (Allen, 1990, as cited in Honeycutt, 2003; Holt & Stone, 1988).

Although relational satisfaction and commitment have been proposed as the force holding LDDRs together, both satisfaction and commitment LDDRs co-occur with idealization. Schwebel et al. (1992) found that relational satisfaction among college students prior to separation in the fall was strongly related to the survival of the relationship throughout the school term. Individuals in long-distance dating relationships report a greater belief that their relationships will work out in the long run (Van Horn et al., 1997) or that they will marry at some point in the future (Stafford, 2004; Stafford & Reske, 1990) than their geographically close counterparts. Individuals in LDDRs also report a greater "moral burden" to continue the relationship than proximal partners and moral commitment has been found to be correlated with relationship stability (Lydon, Pierce, & O'Regan, 1997). However, increased investments and commitment has been found to lead to increased positive relational distortion (Rusbult et al., 2001), thus idealization may still be the mechanism maintaining these relationships.

In short, constrained communication appears to promote positive illusions, and positive illusions have been found to promote premarital stability (Murray & Holmes, 1996). However, there is little debate that interaction is necessary to acquire knowledge about one's partner, and "depth of acquaintance" has remained a consistent predictor of later marital quality and stability (Larson & Holman, 1994). "People need to spend sufficient time before marriage developing essential processes that will enhance their marriage" (Cate et al., 2002, p. 262). Couples who avoid conflict in premarital stages of relationships are subsequently at risk (Gottman & Krokoff, 1989). Everyday casual interaction can provide a safe context within which more specific discussions can occur and partners can learn about one another (Duck, 1990). Everyday casual interaction is sorely lacking in LDDRs. Though an often repeated finding is that the length of dating prior to marriage is associated with marital stability (Cate et al., 2002; Larson & Holman, 1994), it is undoubtedly not the passage of time per se that is important, but rather the interaction which takes place during this time. LDDRs survive and even thrive without this interaction raising concerns about future stability and satisfaction.

BECOMING GEOGRAPHICALLY CLOSE

Although individuals fear that separation may result in relational termination (Van Horn et al., 1997), minimal consideration has been given to the possibility of termination when long-distance couples become geographically close. To the extent that idealization held the couple together, the couple may be at risk for termination as overly idealized images may be difficult to maintain when day-to-day reality ensues.

Little is known about what happens when LDDRs become proximal. Preliminary results from a sample of approximately 100 long-distance dating individuals who subsequently moved to the same geographic location reveals that many individuals espouse desirable aspects of their long-distance status that they missed when moving to the same location (Stafford et al., 2004). Some individuals reported missing the freedom and autonomy to spend time with friends, on homework or jobs, or other activities, and the novelty or excitement of a LDDR. Of course, the expense or hassle of traveling was not missed, although some individuals actually reported increased expense; they now had to spend more money on dates. Spending FtF time appears to increase; so does conflict. Ironically, some report missing the feeling of missing each other or of anticipation of seeing each other; now permanently together the relationship was no longer interesting or exciting. In fact, LDDRs are likely to terminate on reunion as during separation (Stafford et al.).

Stafford et al., (2004) also found that some individuals indicated adjusting to each other and becoming aware of previously unknown aspects of their partner or relationship. Issues in adjusting or learning about each other were sometimes positive, other times negative, and sometimes were simple statements of fact. For example, some reported that they had not truly appreciated how wonderful their partner was until they came together full time, that they become emotionally closer, and enjoyed their increased FtF time. Others reported discovering personality flaws that had remained hidden while apart, or realizing they did not truly know the other person when they were apart. Some now felt smothered. Also prevalent were statements that the relationship was just as they expected it to be.

Stafford et al. also found a few couples terminated the relationship within a few days of permanently moving to the same location, and several relationships lasted only 1 or 2 months on uniting, even after a much longer time of being a couple in separate locations. Others were still together well over a year after uniting.

In short, moving to the same location invoked a wide range or responses, including relational termination for some and escalation for others. More-over, the various factors that might be influential in transitioning to proximal couples, such as length of time dating prior to separation and length of sepa-ration were not predictive of relational demise when becoming proximal (Stafford et al., 2004).

RELATIONAL DEMISE AS SUCCESS

A criterion of relational stability as success is simplistic at best. Adding other rela-tional features generally considered positive, such as commitment or satisfaction, is not much better. Much ado is made of communication as necessary for relational development, with minimal accord granted to the possibility that increased inter-action may result in increased knowledge and subsequent relational demise. Due to the restricted interaction, romanticized images of each other prevail in conjunc-tion with overly positive self-presentations cyclically feeding into each other's ro-manticized images. Thus, long-distance partners "may have little idea of how idealized and inaccurate their images are" (Stafford & Reske, 1990, p. 278).

Stafford and Reske (1990) expressed misgivings over young adults making decisions regarding long-term commitments such as marriage in this idealized and unknowingly uninformed state. Concern is not with general positive per-ceptions of one's partner, but rather with potential critical inaccuracies derived by completing visions of one's partner or relationship from one's own mental prototype rather than based on information about the specific partner. In addi-tion, previously masked areas of irreconcilable differences will inevitably sur-face when together on a daily basis. Given their limited interactions, long-distance couples may not be truly gaining knowledge about their partner in or-der to make informed decisions about marriage (Stafford et al., 2004).

Certainly some dating, in U.S. culture, is purely recreational. However, when dating is operating as mate selection, it may be likened to an extended inter-view process to determine if the two individuals are indeed suited. Long-dis-tance dating partners should be urged to develop deeper relational knowledge and in doing so "couples will either address areas in which they differ or termi-nate the relationship" (Stafford & Reske, 1990, p. 278). Either outcome is seen as a success, although it is unlikely the relational partners will see the latter as success, at least not immediately. However, it has been said, "the best divorce is one you get before you get married" (Hill, Rubin, & Peplau, 1976).

CONCLUSIONS

Individuals in LDDRs may be especially prone to idealized, inaccurate views of their partners. Romanticized visions and over-projections of similarity have generally been thought to occur in early stages of relationships and then dissipate with increased interaction. Distance may not allow for this dissipation.

No argument is made that idealized images should be avoided or abandoned, nor are they unique to LDDRs. On the contrary, "benevolent misconceptions" (Ickes & Simpson, 1997) protect even geographically close relationships. A certain amount of misunderstanding or optimistic adoration may well be necessary for the preservation of relationships in general (Sillars, 1998). Of course all of us want our relationships to be superior to others' relationships (Rusbult et al., 2000).

Positive illusions in and of themselves are not problematic. They have long been thought to be an important element of courtship (Waller, 1937). Furthermore, some idealization may be necessary to enter into long-term commitments and to sustain our relationships (Sabetelli, 1988). A conundrum exists in finding a balance between functional idealistic distortion and problematic perceptual inaccuracies. Seeing our romantic partners through rose colored glasses has many benefits (Hendrick & Hendrick, 1988). However, "it hardly seems pragmatic to gloss over the faults of a *potential* romantic partner" (Goodwin, Fiske, Rosen, & Rosenthal, 2002, p. 232, italics in original).

5

Adult Romantic Relationships

Heterosexual long-distance marriages inform most of the research in this chapter as research on other long-distance adult romantic relationships is limited. Ideally, this chapter would also consider the long-distance family as a holistic entity including children when applicable; unfortunately, partners who live apart and their children are seldom studied simultaneously. In general, children are taken into account only secondarily in terms of how their age or mere existence affects long-distance romantic couples. The exception is research on the effects of parental absence on the child and, to some extent, family role adaptations.

As noted in the introductory chapter, most sociological definitions of marriage include a shared residence (Rindfuss & Stephen, 1990). Nonetheless, the U.S. Census Bureau estimates that about 2.8 million married persons live apart for reasons other than martial discord or consideration of divorce (Fields & Casper, 2001). This is likely an underestimate of married partners who routinely enact their relationships from a distance. For example, couples who do not technically live apart but spend a significant amount of time away from each other because of travel are not included in the Census classification. "A person was classified [by the Census Bureau] as 'married, spouse present' if the husband or wife was reported as a member of the household, even though he or she may have been temporarily absent on business" (U.S. Census Bureau, 2002). Researchers have often invoked broader criteria considering married couples who spend at least 3 nights per week apart as long distance (Gerstel & Gross, 1984). Given the number of married individuals who live apart for numerous reasons, aside from consideration of divorce, cohabitation should not be assumed to be a defining characteristic of marriage: it should be a variable within marriage (Rindfuss & Stephen, 1990). Similarly, given the rise in nonmarital cohabitation, marriage might be considered a variable within committed unions. For some individuals, marriage is not desired; for others, it is not a legal option (e.g., homosexuals, though this is currently being debated in the courts). Moreover, some couples, though married, voluntarily choose to live apart (e.g., dual-career couples); for others, separation is involuntary, as in the case of incarceration. In short, marriage and cohabitation should be considered separate constructs.

This chapter delineates forms of adult romantic LDRs, criteria for success, and the presence of stress. Relational maintenance, reunions, and societal support for the long-distance family are then discussed.

TYPES OF LONG-DISTANCE ADULT UNIONS

A multiplicity of variations of long-distance committed unions among adults exists. Most research has considered heterosexual married couples. Even within that parameter a plurality of circumstances surrounding separations is found. These include dual-career couples, single-residence marriages that require one or both spouses to spend extensive time away from home, military deployments, and incarceration. In addition, research is just beginning to emerge on unmarried, committed adult relationships; these partners may be separated for any of the same reasons as married partners.

The first global type of long-distance marriage or family is dual career, dual residence (DCDR). These arrangements refer to married individuals, with or without children, who voluntarily maintain two distinct residences, intend to stay married, and are both committed to careers. The partners choose to live separately because of difficulties finding suitable career opportunities in the same geographic location (Anderson & Spruill, 1993; Gross, 1980; Taylor & Lounsbury, 1988). Estimates place the number of DCDR couples in the United States at around 700,000 (Maines, 1993) to 1 million (Stroh, 1999).

Research on DCDR couples peaked during the late 1970s to mid-1980s (Douvan & Pleck, 1978; Farris, 1978; Gerstel, 1978, 1979; Gerstel & Gross, 1982, 1983, 1984, 1987; Govaerts & Dixon, 1988; Johnson, 1987; Kirschner & Walum, 1978; Winfield, 1985). However, interest may be re-emerging (see Magnuson & Norem, 1999; Rhodes, 2002).

The lack of recent research on DCDR marriages is surprising given the large number of dual-career academicians. Approximately 40% of academic women are married to academic partners, which results in many DCDR marriages (Astin & Milem, 1997). The situation is so prevalent that physicists and other scientists have punfully labeled the dual-career problem the "dual-body" problem (McNeil & Sher, 1999).

The second global type of long-distance marriage is civilian single-residence, single-career families. In these instances one partner, typically the wife, remains at the primary residence as the occupational demands of the other require extended absence. Though not discussed in the literature, with the number of women in the labor force there are likely circumstances when both spouses spend a significant amount of time away from home. Some occupations such as professional athletes, politicians, merchant marines, and selected business professions require routine separations (Gerstel & Gross, 1984). These separations might be regular, frequent, and short, such as business professionals who are gone for several days a week (Boss, McCubbin, & Lester, 1979; Roehling & Bultman, 2002). Separations in other professions, such as offshore oil workers, can be for months at a time (Lowenstein, 1986; Morrice & Taylor, 1978; Vormbrock, 1993).

Despite popular interest in high-profile celebrity bi-coastal couples, the two most common reasons for marital noncohabitation are military service[4] and incarceration[5] (Rindfuss & Stephen, 1990). In 2000, the United States had approximately 2 million individuals in federal, state, or local prisons (Bureau of Justice Statistics, 2003).

Though separations accompanying military life and the ramifications of separations on military families have a long research tradition (e.g., see Waller, 1940), interest is increasing as the number of military personnel with spouses and children has risen dramatically. For example, 16% of Vietnam soldiers were married with children, compared with 60% of Gulf War soldiers (Military Family Resource Center, 2002). During the time of the ongoing Iraqi conflict, 58% of active duty military personnel are married or have children, or both (NCFR, 2004).

Two additional types of long-distance romantic relationships have escaped much study. The first is the long-distance nonmarital cohabiting couple. Although this may seem oxymoronic, such couples are those who have cohabited without marriage and then moved to separate geographic vicinities, not because of discord or intent to dissolve the union but for career or educational reasons. A cohabitating couple may resume coresidence with or without marriage (Binstock & Thornton, 2003). The extent to which studies of long-distance dating relationships or marriages include prior cohabiters is unknown, as information about prior cohabitation is generally not reported.

---

[4]A subset of military personnel separated from their families is POWs and MIAs. Obviously these family members experience stresses and strains different from most other long-distance families, including a greater uncertainty of eventual return and legal complications unmatched by those with an absent, yet accounted for, spouse or parent. Given that the focus here is on communication, and communication with such individuals is almost always impossible, research surrounding MIAs and POWs is not reviewed here. This is meant in no way to lessen the importance of research on and practical ways to aid families in this situation (see Campbell & Demi, 2000; McCubbin, Dahl, Lester, Benson, & Robertson, 1976).
[5]Interaction with family members of incarcerated individuals on death row is not considered here. These family members face prolonged and distorted grief, with no societally accepted modes of mourning. They encounter extreme senses of guilt, isolation, and feelings of powerlessness and psychological problems (Smykla, 1987).

Another type of couple not formally recognized nor researched in the United States is living-apart-together (LAT) couples. The defining characteristic of an LAT couple is the desire for a committed union unaccompanied by full-time coresidential status. LAT couples may or may not be married, may be heterosexual or homosexual, might or might not have children, are self-defined as a couple, and both partners have their own primary residence (Levin & Trost, 1999). LAT couples exist for many reasons beyond career concerns, military duty, or incarceration. For example, members of a union formed later in life may desire to retain separate homes to live in proximity to children or grandchildren (see Levin & Trost, 1999, for a review of types of and reasons for LAT couples).

SUCCESS

As with dating couples, the most prevalent conception of a successful marriage, or other romantic union, is one that remains intact. Also like dating couples, attributes such as satisfaction and commitment are often considered as success. From an ecological systemic perspective (Bronfenbrenner, 1979), individuals, families, networks, and the larger society in which they are located are all interrelated, yet each of these has its own definition of success. Thus, to consider success only as stability or satisfaction misses much of the picture of LDRs. For the individual, success may entail coping with stress due to separations. For corporations or the military, successful LDRs are those that result in job retention and superior job performance. Even society has a yardstick for success; for example, relationships with an incarcerated family member might be considered successful if maintaining relationships lowers recidivism rates.

Stability and Satisfaction

Rindfuss and Stephen (1990) found that within the first 3 years after separation, noncohabitating spouses have a divorce rate twice that of cohabitating spouses. These conclusions were drawn largely from military personnel and incarcerated individuals, both of whom have higher divorce rates than the population at large. Research is silent on the divorce or dissolution of couples who live apart for other reasons, such as DCDR couples.

The literature does provide a general profile of satisfied DCDR marriages. Available data indicate that successful DCDR couples hold less traditional and more egalitarian sex roles, are well educated, and engage in planning and joint decision making about the separation (Anderson & Spruill, 1993; Forsyth & Gramling, 1987). Gerstel (1978) found the best fit of career cycle and family life cycle occurs mid-career after children have left home. However, most DCDR couples are in relatively early stages, and approximately 50% have children living at home (Anderson & Spruill, 1993; Forsyth & Gramling, 1987). Those with greater financial resources or flexible job schedules experience fewer difficulties (Anderson, 1992). In addition, the more difficult and trying the commute, the greater is the dissatisfaction with the lifestyle (Groves & Horm-Wingerd, 1991). Roehling and Bultman (2002) found that marital satisfaction among individuals in DCDR couples differed depending both on spouses' gender role attitudes and on which spouse traveled. Yet, a deficit of longitudinal research on DCDR marriages exists.

Although divorce among military populations may be higher than the population at large, divorces seldom occur during deployment itself. Also, divorce rates are higher among military personnel who have returned from deployments than among those who have not been deployed. Divorces spiked upon the demobilization following World War II (DaVanzo & Rahman, 1993). Angrist and Johnson (2000) found that male deployments were not related to divorce following the Gulf War, but female deployments were. For deployed women, the longer the deployment the greater the chance of divorce with each month of deployment, raising the probability of divorce by about 1.4% (Angrist & Johnson, 2000). All deployments are not the same. There is some evidence that combat experience especially hurts marital relationships (Gimbel & Booth, 1994).

Stress of Separation

DCDR couples are assumed to experience greater stress and dissatisfaction than single-residence dual-career couples (Bunker, Zubek, Vanderslice, & Rice, 1992). This has not been substantiated. On the contrary, DCDR couples may be the most likely LDR form to reap benefits; they are voluntarily separated precisely for the benefits they hope to incur.[6] In current U.S. culture, marriages are concurrently supposed to provide individual self-fulfillment and growth as well as intense emotional intimacy (Cate & Lloyd, 1992). DCDR marriages, in theory, allow for both.

Though certainly not applicable to all people, the predominant relational philosophy in the United States is an individualistic view of selves; relationships exist to meet individual needs (Gergen, 1991). The major benefit of DCDR arrangements are career opportunities. Dual residences allow independence, time, and flexibility to focus on careers, thus meeting desires for personal fulfillment (Groves & Horm-Wingerd, 1991). Segmentation of personal lives and ca-

---

[6]Voluntary is subjective. These relationships are referred to here as voluntary as no higher authority, such as the government or one's parents, dictates their separations. Gerstel and Gross (1984) pointed out that individuals within DCDR marriages may not feel that their separations are voluntary; they may perceive no other options as viable.

reers is common. Work is prioritized when apart, and family is prioritized when together (Gerstel & Gross, 1984).

Bunker et al. (1992) found DCDR couples to be more satisfied with their work than dual-career, single-residence couples. In the only located study of an African American sample of DCDR couples, a stated benefit of their arrangement was combating racial stereotypes and racial oppression as the geographic separation allowed them to pursue higher level, higher paying jobs than seeking jobs in the same location would have allowed (Jackson, Brown, & Patterson-Stewart, 2000).

The intent is not to imply that DCDR relationships are void of any difficulties. Some stress is inevitable in any relationship. However, the severity of stress may be contingent on the factors surrounding the separation, and one major factor for these couples is the presence and age of children. A DCDR arrangement is generally more difficult for couples with children than for those without children (Rotter, Barnett, & Fawcett, 1998). Among families with children, those in later stages of the family cycle (i.e., with older children) fare better than those with younger children (Anderson, 1992). When children are involved, the marital relationship becomes less egalitarian and more like a dual-career single-residence couple, as the children live in one home that serves as the primary residence (Rotter et al., 1998). The partner living away from the children is able to focus more on career, and the partner residing with the children, usually the mother, becomes in many ways like a single parent. She is faced with practical child care arrangements and is less able to focus on her career. Thus, the primary benefit of entering the arrangement is predominately lost for her. In such cases resentment often results (Rhodes, 2002). There are costs for the commuting parent as well. Traveling parents report missing the day-to-day aspects of their children's development and suffering feelings of guilt. Viewing the separation as short term and best for the family in the long run alleviates some of these feelings (Rhodes, 2002; Rotter et al., 1998).

Unlike assumptions concerning college students and DCDR couples, the symptoms of distress are well documented among the families of deployed military personnel and single-resident civilian families with extended separations. Families with an incarcerated member face much stress as well. In all of these families, the at-home partner commonly encounters severe depression, loneliness, role changes and overload, financial concerns, and increased parenting demands with diminished parenting abilities. The at-home spouse may experience a wide range of emotions including worry about the absent partner, detachment, and resentment (see Vormbrock, 1993, for a review). The term *submariners' wives syndrome* has been coined by psychiatrists to refer to such dysphoric symptoms accompanying long-term separations (Isay, 1968). Husband or father distress during women's absence has received minimal attention; the little existing research on women's absence has been primarily on the effects of their absence on children (see chap. 5, this volume).

Additional stresses for military families include frustration with bureaucracy and fears about safety (Drummet, Coleman, & Cable, 2003; Hunter, 1982). Family members of incarcerated individuals report similar strains, with the added burdens of stigmatization and lack of support (Hairston, 1991). For these individuals, concern is not with the fulfillment of career goals but often simply the ability to make it through the day.

RELATIONAL MAINTENANCE

The proposal has been offered that some people maintain completely satisfactory relationships, with virtually no FtF interaction for several months, but that relationships require at least some FtF connect as "extremely infrequent contact probably does ultimately result in relationship instability" (Guldner & Swenson, 1995, p. 319). Yet, infrequent FtF contact is normative for many romantic partners. Months of separation occur in some civilian occupations and typify military deployment. Incarcerations can last for years.

As mentioned earlier, limited research on adult nonmilitary romantic partners exists, aside from a brief period of interest in the 1970s through the mid-1980s (See Gerstel & Gross, 1984; Winfield, 1985). This literature seldom focuses directly on considerations of communication or maintenance. Most of the extant knowledge on contact in long-distance romantic unions is informed by military research and thus serves as the primary basis of this section. The military's concern is of little surprise as it has a vested interest in spousal satisfaction. Spousal satisfaction greatly influences soldiers' morale and re-enlistment (Rosen & Moghadam, 1988).

FtF Contact

Consistent with the societal emphasis on FtF contact, the military has attempted allowing physical copresence during deployment. Spousal visits to bases for a few days during peacetime have been tried; these were found to be of questionable, if any, benefit. Some partners actually saw each other very little during their visits because of the soldier's assignments. Thus, morale for both was lowered (Carlson & Carlson, 2002).

Conclusions are mixed about mid-deployment, or rest and recuperation (R&R), leaves. The R&R program came into full swing again about 7 months after the beginning of the recent Iraqi conflict. However, many troops have been denied these opportunities as priority is granted to providing relief for ground troops (McEntee, 2003). For those able to take leave, it is about 2 weeks, but with travel time visits are less than 10 days. Spouses are overwhelmingly in support of the program, though the visit can be unsettling after months of separation. Such leaves have been found to be especially difficult for young children to understand. The rapid and brief contact can inflict more emotional or psychological trauma on all involved than the initial separation. Overall, studies have shown that following such leaves depression and stress levels tend to increase and desire to stay in the military decreases (Bell, Bartone, Bartone, Schumm, & Gade, 1997). In addition, families dislike the lack of control over when the visits are scheduled, the lack of advance notice about the visit, and the fact they are not compensatory.

Mediated Contact

The greatest desire during deployments for both military personnel and spouses is for increased access to communication through telephone and e-mail, and military personnel are beginning to expect the availability of such contact (Ross, 2001). Military personnel reported the inability to engage in regular communication as a contributing factor to feeling less intimacy with their partner (Jacobs & Hicks, 1987). Soldiers who experienced "satisfaction with resources to communicate home" were more positively adjusted than "those who experienced dissatisfaction with communication resources" (Rohall, Segal, & Segal, 1999, p. 59). In other words, "soldiers who feel that they are able to communicate more readily with the families find it [the separation] less difficult" (p. 59), regardless of whether they actually take advantage of the communication opportunities; knowledge of the availability of means for interaction may be more important for peace of mind than actual use of those means.

Reports are mixed about telephone use among deployed soldiers in Bosnia (Pincus, House, Christenson, & Adler, 2001). For some spouses at home, phone calls can provide a "stabilizing experience." The calls themselves, which allow the family members to connect briefly, are likely more important than the content. They signify reassurance and the existence of the relationship, and seem to be beneficial if the conversations are simply to stay in touch or to recognize special days such as birthdays and anniversaries (Pincus et al., 2001).

Conversely, other spouses and soldiers reported having predominantly bad phone calls that only made things worse (Pincus & Nam, 1999). Phone contact allows the increased opportunities for conflict (Pincus et al., 2001). Caution has been urged about recent considerations of equipping soldiers with cell phones (Pincus et al., 2001): The "disadvantage of easy phone access is the immediacy and proximity to unsettling events at home or in theater" (p. 23). Other problems included frustration by the home spouse as the phone contact can only be initiated by military personnel. Spouses report feeling confined to the house as they might miss a call, given they have little or no prediction when or if a call will be placed. If indeed the spouse is not home when a call is attempted, soldiers report feelings of abandonment and isolation. Limited work on DCDR couples report similar mixed feelings about telephone use. Some commuters report that phone calls make them feel more connected; others report that phone calls increase loneliness and inability to focus on their jobs (Gerstel & Gross, 1984).

Unlike phone calls, letters have been associated with relational satisfaction. Naval spouses and deployed naval personnel reported higher marital satisfaction with letters than with phone calls. Letters can be edited by the writer to avoid the delivery of upsetting or negative information; they tend to contain more positive emotional tones and are often reassuring in a vague and supportive manner (Stafford & Yost, 1990).

Pincus et al. (2001) proposed that e-mail may be a better method of communication among deployed families than telephone contact, as timing is not an issue. Moreover, as with letters, one can edit and reread e-mail to "filter out intense emotions that may be unnecessarily disturbing" (Pincus et al., 2001, p. 24). However, Ross (2001) found the benefits of e-mail to be equivocal in a study of naval personnel. Approximately one half of both sailors and spouses reported that e-mail did not meet their expectations. Ross's overall conclusion was that e-mail increased the quality of life for some families but expectations for e-mail availability were related to morale problems when systems were down or unavailable.

Symbolic Contact and Cognitive Connections

Military families have been advised to maintain a "partner-aware" orientation (Van Breda, 1999). The at-home family members actively strive to maintain the symbolic presence of the absent family member. This might involve family rituals to bring to mind the absent spouse or parent and thus nurture feelings of connection (Imber-Black & Roberts, 1992). Rituals create feelings of comfort and security. Such strategies have been met with success in clinical samples of naval couples (Van Breda, 1999).

Cognitive connections take place in the minds of the absent partner as well. For example, engaging in any type of contact with incarcerated individuals is often difficult: Phone calls are expensive; visits may be logistically impossible because of the geographic distance or the expense of traveling. Yet, holding onto positive memories of relational histories, with little to no interaction, buffers incarcerated individuals against a sense of loneliness (Segrin & Flora, 2001). See chapter 10, this volume, for more on cognitive connections.

NEGOTIATING REUNIONS

Regardless of the reason for separation, most individuals look forward to reunions. Like college students (see chap. 4, this volume), long-distance dual-career and single-residence couples have high expectations about the quality of their time together when they reunite, as do deployed military personnel (Bell & Schumm, 2000; Gross, 1980). Those with frequent, predictable, and short separations, often experience a honeymoon-like reunion, putting their best fronts on, and avoiding conflict, similar to long-distance dating couples (Gerstel & Gross, 1984; Vormbrock, 1993).

The experience is different for those with long-term separations. When couples are separated for extended periods of time, idealization often re-emerges. Positive illusions both serve to sustain a relationship as well as to promote potentially damaging, overly high expectations. Reintegration into the relational and family dynamics involves redefining roles, power structures, and boundary regulations and often encountering unmet expectations. Reunions are tumultuous.

Hill (1945, 1949, 1958) was the first to identify and discuss patterns or stages during the military deployment cycle. Hill (1958) described the deployment cycle as a roller-coaster-like ride. Hill was also the first to examine coping behaviors of the spouse at home during deployment. At that time the at-home spouse was almost exclusively the wife, and sex roles were fairly traditional in these military families.

He identified three patterns. Some women held onto traditional sex roles and attempted to adapt without making substantive adjustments. The family was in turmoil as these women felt helpless and incapable of operating without their husbands' input, which was generally impossible to gain. At the other extreme, in some families' husbands were excluded psychologically and his roles and duties were divided among children, the wife, and extended family. This family appeared to function well in the deployed soldier's absence. However, the family encountered the most traumatic readjustment upon his return. Hill's third pattern was most successful. These families included the father symbolically and psychologically, and continued affectionate contact through regular letters. The mother made decisions and exercised power and authority in the father's absence. These families did experience more difficulty with the father's absence than did families that shut the father out entirely, but they also experienced fewer difficulties adjusting to the father's reintegration into the family.

Role adjustments continue to be a source of difficulty for today's military families. Roles, routines, authority, and power structures must all be renegotiated upon spouse's departure, arrival, and redeployment. The returning solider unrealistically expects everything to be the same as predeployment; is surprised to find many duties were reassigned to extended family, the spouse, or children; and often experiences boredom and restlessness after a brief period (Wood, Scarville, & Gravino, 1995). The spouse who remains at home may desire admiration or appreciation for successfully accomplishing family tasks, yet discovers the military partner wants to resume these tasks. The at-home spouse then reports feeling resentful and unappreciated (Wood et al., 1995).

Forsyth and Gramling (1987) offered a summary of coping patterns based on both military and long-term civilian separations. Their findings are remarkably similar to Hill's (1945, 1949, 1958) reports decades earlier, and again the away partner is most often male. Forsyth and Gramling noted that the occupations requiring prolonged separations tend be working-class families who generally adhere to traditional sex role power and authority structures. Like Hill, Forsyth and Gramling's conclusion is that prolonged separations disrupt this power structure, and thus family dynamics revolve around adaptation to changing roles.

Forysth and Gramling (1987) reported five types of patterns. The first is the "replacement husband/father." During times of absence, a male or males from the extended family act as the base of power and authority. Another type of adaptation process occurs with "contingent authority." The wife takes on the husband's traditional authority in limited areas during his absence; she remains traditional in most ways. The children develop quite a bit of power given the wife's discomfort in the role as disciplinarian. A third type of adaptation is "alternating authority." Here, power and authority are passed back and forth between husband and wife. She does act as the decision maker, disciplinarian, and the family authority in his absence, but these roles are handed over to the father on his return. Forsyth and Gramling noted that this is most common when separations are short and predictable. The fourth pattern is one characterized by conflict. The mother takes on the same roles as in the alternating authority model; then does not relinquish the roles on the father's return. Conflict ensues as the father expects to resume his place. The last family type portrayed is that of the father as "periodic guest." In this case, the mother takes on all the of roles of the traditional mother and father (aside from primary wage earner). The father's reunion is anticipated and enjoyed, at first. However, his presence becomes difficult and problematic as he disrupts the family system that has emerged; they have settled into roles, routines, social networks, and activities that do not include him. The mother–children subsystem boundaries often merge as she has come to rely on and consult the children about household concerns. In essence, the father is a guest in his own home and, after a while, anxiously awaits his next departure.

Though these patterns may operate during cycles of coming and going, they do not inform us about adaptation upon the permanent return of the father to the family home or how to facilitate relationships in his absence. In addition, how the patterns might vary among individuals who do not follow traditional male-dominant role structures or may extend to women as absent partners is unknown.

SOCIETAL SUPPORT

Support from the proximal community and society at large varies considerably among long-distance romantic relationships. DCDR marriages may encounter less societal support than dating couples given that norms for marital coresidence are stronger than norms for dating couple proximity. "Social disapproval ... is seen by most sociologists and psychologists as the most difficult problem the DCDR couple has to face" (Winfield, 1985, p. 168). Similarly, Bunker et al. (1992) reported that popular images of the families living apart are "generally pessimistic" (p. 339). As a result, they speculated that such families may limit contact with community to avoid such explicit or implicit criticism. The limited contact in turn reduces potential support networks for child care and other practical problems. Indeed, Gerstel and Gross (1984) found that neither personal networks, the workplace, nor society in general supported DCDR marriages. The wisdom of such a nonconventional lifestyle is questioned (Gerstel & Gross, 1984), and friends and family members often perceive the decision to reside apart as a lack of interest in or commitment to the marriage and as an early warning sign of an impending divorce (Groves & Horm-Wingerd, 1991). However, Groves and Horm-Wingerd (1991) also found that although society at large is not accepting of the lack of coresidence among married partners, on a case by case basis, family and friends may provide comfort and support.

Although not examined in conjunction with long-distance marriages, evidence indicates that network overlap is related to marital satisfaction (Milardo & Helms-Erikson, 2000). By default, individuals in long-distance marriages have less network overlap. In addition, DCDR couples are also less likely to know individuals in similar situations than couples in college dating relationships or military personnel. The picture of societal support for DCDR marriages is a bleak one, although arguably they are in less need of community support than many other types of LDRs given their relatively high incomes and ease of contact compared with families with an incarcerated member, military families, or many single-career families.

Unlike most other forms of LDRs, military personnel and their families have institutionalized support systems (Norwood, Fullerton, & Hagen, 1996). The military has numerous family support services and attempts to involve families in these programs. Much of this support is emotional. Some is instrumental, such as providing group day care or car maintenance (Reed & Segal, 2000). Support may come in terms of information or services directly from the military or through facilitation of connections among families of military, such as coordinating support groups. Calling trees among spouses to disseminate information and to raise awareness of military support systems and opportunities have also been organized by military command (Norwood et al., 1996).

Communication from the military unit to the spouse appears to alleviate marital distress; thus, dissemination of information by the military is another form of assistance. Military units may send out newsletters or other publications providing information about current activities, attempting to control rumors, and providing practical suggestions for spouses and children (Rose, Durand, Westhuis, & Teitelbaum, 1995).

Dissemination of information and connections with other military family members can be especially helpful for younger, more recently married spouses facing their first deployment, as well as civilian husbands and reservists as they tend to be the least integrated into military life and thus know the least about support opportunities but are the most at risk (Black, 1993; Knox & Price, 1995).

Although community support appears beneficial (Rosen & Moghadam, 1988), today's military is faced with the problem of maintaining a sense of military community. Approximately 70% of active duty military families live in civilian communities as opposed to military communities (Defense Manpower Data Center, 2003). Of those families who were living on base before a spouse's overseas deployment, many move away from the base during the deployment (Schumm, Bell, & Knott, 2000). These families have decreased connections and cohesion with other military families. Therefore, an increasing challenge for the military is to develop means to supply information to these families and encourage involvement in military support systems (Ursano & Norwood, 1996).

Given the dispersion of the military community, even though more services are offered today than ever before, the spouse is simultaneously more in need of comfort and assistance from the civilian community. Disadvantages for the spouse and the military can result as families off-base have decreased access to information and military support groups.

However, living off-base is not necessarily detrimental. Many spouses choose to move closer to relatives for instrumental support as well as emotional support. This can actually benefit both the family and the military (Bell & Schumm, 1999). Often, military spouses attribute successful separations to their local social support networks of friends, family, and church communities, rather than military networks (Wood et al., 1995). Spouses and families who weather separations best rely on a combination of formal and informal military networks, formal civilian support programs, backing from their own employers, and informal assistance of friends and family (Martin & McClure, 2000).

A unique form of community support often available to military families is overall societal support; missions that are popularly endorsed or at least understood by the individual's community foster a helpful climate for the family. Deployments not seen as "legitimate," or those that are not popular (e.g., Vietnam), or not well understood (e.g., Somalia) create more difficulties for the spouse at home than those that are endorsed and embraced by society at large (e.g., World War II; Ursano & Norwood, 1996).

Although support for military spouses and children may ebb and flow with society's views of the specific deployment, families separated because of incarceration, despite their readily apparent needs, receive virtually no community support, institutional or otherwise. For the most part, they encounter quite the opposite. Families with an incarcerated member often become isolated because of lack of institutional, community or family support resources (Western

& McLanahan, 2000). They also incur social stigma, lack of sympathy, involuntary single parenting, and poverty (Arditti, Lambert-Shute, & Joest, 2003). Like military families, family members of incarcerated individuals have difficulty in acquiring both information about policies and practices of the bureaucratic system and information about their family member (Hairston, 2001b). Uncertainty about rules and policies and uncertainty about their incarcerated member's status are predominant concerns (Fishman, 1990). This information deficit is encountered both because of a lack of easily accessible information (Hairston, 2001b) and because of the family's discomfort or embarrassment in turning to others for information (Arditti et al., 2003).

Families with an incarcerated member have few formal resources to use. Some do not seek public assistance because of lack of information about the assistance; others are suspicious of formal organizations (Beckerman, 1994). Some states offer programs designed to provide support to these families. These programs range from instrumental help, such as providing food and clothing, to facilitating contact among the incarcerated prisoners and family members, to emotional help such as aiding the formation of support groups. Psychological intervention for children of incarcerated parents is another form of support. Many programs are geared at facilitating visitation itself. Services include provision of information concerning visitation policies, intervention concerning problems with visitation, facilitation of more family-friendly visits, and payment for visits of children. Such programs are rare and poorly funded.

According to Arditti et al. (2003), the most likely successful arena of intervention among for prisoners' families is "enhancing naturally occurring networks of support for these families" (p. 202). The provision of social support alleviates some emotional distresses, helps reduce isolation, increases parenting abilities, and often prevents poverty. Despite the potential individual and societal benefits, such support is seldom enacted.

Most contend that community support and involvement are beneficial for virtually all types of LDR couples and families, yet Vormbrock (1993), operating from attachment theory, cautioned against too much proximal support. She concluded from her review of numerous types of long-distance marriages that individuals in relationships with routine long separations can become overly reliant on proximal social support. This excess dependency on physically close family and community blurs boundaries and roles, and makes reunion more difficult. Family members at home may have fewer immediate difficulties and may be distracted from their loneliness through such involvements. However, Vormbrock reported that some individuals become less attached and less emotionally involved with the absent member over time. This detachment feeds a cycle of continued reasons to stay apart and decreased reliance on and attachment to the absent member. This is reminiscent of the patterns identified by Forsyth and Gramling (1987), wherein returning members feel like guests in their own homes and look forward to departing again. The proximal network can dysfunctionally enable psychological and emotional separation as opposed to enhancing the relationship of the physically separated family members.

CONCLUSIONS

It is obvious that there is no immediate answer to the question of how to make long-distance arrangements successful. Success may even be defined on a variety of levels. Ironically, many factors that allow for successful coping, such as becoming more independent, recalling one's partner and relationship idealistically, and turning to local support networks, result in more difficult reunions. Furthermore, it cannot be assumed that all long-distance romantic arrangements have more difficulties or stressors than geographically close ones. Recall that in instances of voluntary noncohabitation, some individuals prefer the arrangement to continue indefinitely.

Regarding communication per se, the desire for more contact among separated individuals appears to be virtually universal. Nonetheless, it remains to be seen if increasing frequency of interaction is beneficial. The possibility is raised that DCDR marriages can reach a point of too much contact, thus interfering with the reason for separation: segmentation, to focus on their careers. During military separations, too much contact may actually be detrimental for all involved.

Restricted interaction, especially if coupled with negative family adaptation patterns or too much proximal dependency may result in distance and detachment. Yet, individuals in LDDRs, DCDR marriages, and military marriages all report feeling let down or depressed after significant phone time or FtF visits.

Dialectical dilemmas are evident. All involved must balance independence with connection and stability with change. In addition, positive distortions may contribute to relational maintenance, but when expectations diverge too far from the reality encountered on reunion, dissatisfaction inevitably follows.

6

Young Children and Parents

As stated in chapter 5, many individuals in civilian and military occupations spend significant amounts of time away from their children. Children may also live away from one parent because of divorce or nonmarital childbirth. Long-distance parent–child relationships also occur when a parent is imprisoned, whether or not the child's parents have a continuing romantic involvement. In all of these cases, a child has restricted communication opportunities with at least one parent, even if their actual residences are geographically close.

Certainly situations beyond these result in parent–child LDRs, such as placement of children in foster homes or juvenile facilities. However, the relationships considered herein are those that have received the most research attention. By far the most work has been conducted on paternal absence due to divorce.

Just as it is difficult to determine the precise number of couples living apart, it is equally difficult to determine the number of young children with long-distance parents. Some children permanently live separately from one or both parents. In 2000, 28% of children under 18 lived with only one parent: 23% lived with their mothers, 1% lived with their fathers, and 4% lived with neither parent (Fields & Casper, 2001). These statistics include children who have an absent parent due to divorce, nonmarital childbirth, or death. However, the number of children who spend significant periods of time living without one parent due to occupational demands or preferences, military deployment, or incarceration is not represented in reports of children's living arrangements (Fields & Casper, 2001). Thus, the number of children who spend significant portions of their young lives away from at least one parent is grossly underestimated. The cultural assumptions and reasons for these separations are considered.

CULTURAL ASSUMPTIONS AND SUCCESS

Two cultural assumptions are especially relevant to LDRs between parents and young children. First, it is assumed that if parents care about their children, they stay in frequent, FtF contact. This presumption ignores the difficulties of maintaining parent–child bonds when the two do not live together (Leite & McKenry, 2002). There are simply fewer opportunities to be involved in the children's daily lives when living in different households even when geographic proximity is maintained (Amato & Gilbreth, 1999).

Additional obstacles may include uncooperative residential primary caregivers who control access and may even relocate, the related legalities surrounding custody and visitation, and nonresidential parents' own perception of the nature of their roles (Dudley, 1991; Wolchik, Fenaughty, & Braver, 1996). Similar factors influence never-married noncustodial parents; these parents are less likely to be active in their children's lives. Incarcerated parents face a number of logistical, legal, and emotional barriers, including shame or embarrassment. Deployed military fathers are not subjected to the same societal assumptions surrounding divorced dads. Though they have logistical constraints, they do not have the same legal constraints and do not experience the same feelings of shame about their separation as incarcerated parents. Deployed, noncustodial, and incarcerated mothers have the same barriers as fathers, but are more subject to societal disapproval than fathers. In short, society advocates parental involvement with little acknowledgment of the barriers to that involvement.

The second assumption is that frequency of contact between children and a nonresidential parent is good; many investigations track only frequency of contact. The assumption that frequent contact is almost always in the best interest of the child is questioned here. Frequency of contact alone is not a strong predictor of child outcomes or of the strength of the parent–child relationship (Arendell, 1997). Moreover, though not addressed here, the assumption of the benefits of an involved father is most strongly held by highly educated middle-class Whites (Griswold, 1993). This "fatherhood ideal" is not uniformly shared in the United States. Ramifications of the lack of paternal involvement may depend in part on expectations for that involvement.

Long-term socialization is generally considered the benchmark of success (Fitzpatrick & Caughlin, 2002), not the relationship between the parent and the young child per se or the child's immediate happiness. Congruent with this view, most research on children who live apart from a parent has examined the ramifications of the separation on the child's adjustment rather than on the facilitation of positive long-distance (or cross-residential) parent–child relationships.

Much more research on paternal absence has been conducted than on maternal absence and more research has been conducted on permanently nonresident fathers than on temporarily, but frequently absent, fathers. "Children with nonresident fathers are more likely to engage in health-compromising behaviors such as drug and alcohol use, unprotected sex, and cigarette smoking; are less likely to graduate from high school and college; are more likely to experience teenage and/or nonmarital fertility; have lower levels of psychological well-being; have lower earnings; are more likely to be idle (out of school and out of work); and are more likely to experience marital instability in adulthood" (King, Harris, & Heard, 2004, p. 2). However, potential problems are contingent both on the nature of the nonresidential parent–child bond and on the mitigating effects of the involvement of other adults. Moreover, it is open to question whether it is the absence of the father per se that is problematic or the structural aspects, such as poverty and maternal stress, that often result from a lack of parental involvement (see Amato, 2000, for a comprehensive review).

TYPES OF PARENT–YOUNG CHILD SEPARATION

Separation Due to Civilian Occupations

Some children are away from a parent due to DCDR arrangements or other civilian occupations that require significant travel by one parent. As noted in chapter 5, when children are considered in the context of long-distance families, the focus has been more on how their presence or age affects the parents than on how the parental absence affects the children. Other research, presented in chapter 5, has examined children's roles in family coping patterns.

Though approximately 50% of DCDR couples have young children only one study was located that directly examined children's perspectives of their DCDR parents. Jackson et al. (2000) interviewed children of four DCDR families. The children expressed feeling like the traveling parent did not care about them and reported feelings of neglect, anger, and disappointment. On the other hand, children also said they felt unique and important among their peers as they viewed their parents as holding important jobs.

Separation Due to Military Deployment

Approximately 630,000 service members are parents who have 1.3 million children, collectively. The vast majority of children are under age 14 (Military Family Resource Center, 2002). When considering children separated from a parent due to military duties, the presumption is that the deployed parent is the father.

Historically, spouses and primary caregivers of military children have been predominantly women; this remains the case. Most military spouses (96%) are women (Military Family Resource Center, 2002). Thus, more research has been conducted on paternal rather than maternal military duty.

Military children are presumed to be affected both directly by their deployed father's absence and indirectly by their mother's stress and depression that interferes with her parenting abilities (Black, 1993; Schumm, Bell, Knott, & Rice, 1996). Children whose fathers are deployed in times of combat experience more difficulties than those whose fathers are on routine deployments; maternal dysfunction is greater as well, thus indirectly affecting the children (Kelley, Herzog-Simmer, & Harris, 1994).

The number of married women in the military is increasing. The percentage of women in active duty and in the reserves has continued to increase from 1980 to 2001; the proportion of women in the reserves has risen from 6.3% to 17.5%, and the proportion of enlisted women has risen from 8.3% to 14% (Military Family Resource Center, 2002).

The Gulf War became dubbed the "mommy war" as during this conflict 40,793 women were deployed and approximately one third of these had one or more dependent children (Pierce, Vinokur, & Buck, 1998; U.S. Presidential Commission, 1993). Given the rise in maternal deployments, research attention is beginning to turn to child outcomes of maternal absence (Applewhite & Mays, 1996; Kelley et al., 2001).

The number of deployed women is still relatively low, though the controversy surrounding such deployments is high. Concern is not always with the absence of the mother per se, but rather a deficit view of the father; fathers are not seen as able to fulfill adequately the role of primary caregiver by many. Civilian husbands are less likely than civilian wives to live in a military community or to take advantage of military support systems for parents. They are also less likely to take over childcare responsibilities; 74% of deployed men reported the child's mother as primary caregiver while deployed, whereas only 32% of deployed women identified the child's father (Angrist & Johnson, 2000). Despite some controversy, significant differences between children of deployed fathers versus deployed mothers have not been found (Applewhite & Mays, 1996).

During the Gulf War approximately 5,700 dual-military couples were deployed, resulting in many children with both parents deployed (Norwood et al., 1996). Single parents account for approximately 6% of the military (Defense Manpower Data Center, 1999). Children of single parents and those of dual-military parents are considered to be high risk. Children of deployed dual-military parents and single parents change residences to live with extended family members and perhaps change schools and communities, adding to the disruption in their lives (Defense Manpower Data Center, 1999; Martin & McClure, 2000).

Nonresidential Civilian Parents and Their Children

Although a number of children have nonresidential fathers due to nonmarital childbirth and some fathers do have or share custody, research lags behind these societal changes. By far, more research has been conducted on parent–child contact when fathers are nonresidential due to divorce than contact during separation for any other reason.

Most single dads are noncustodial with a wide variety of involvement from no contact to high participation in the child's life. Seltzer (1991) reported that 37% of children of divorced parents had no contact of any kind with their father in a given year. Geographic proximity has been strongly related to parental contact (Cooksey & Craig, 1998). If fathers live too far away for regular visits, they also tend not to communicate by telephone or mail; those who do visit regularly tend to communicate through other modes as well (King & Heard, 1999). Pragmatically, father–child contact is highly correlated with payment of child support among both divorced and never-married fathers (King et al., 2004). Thus, one potential benefit of contact is a lessened probability of poverty.

In addition to proximity, another predictor of father involvement is the father's view of his own role. The quality of contact is related to the role of the father as reciprocally defined by self, society, the mother, and the parental relationship. In the absence of a marital union with the mother, a father who saw his role as parent and husband may have difficulty maintaining a cohesive father–child bond (Kissman, 1997). Restrictions on the amount of time father and children have together and legal limitations given sole maternal custody also play into this role ambiguity. Fathers report feeling like a guest in their children's lives instead of a parent (Arendell, 1997). Thus, their role often disintegrates into an overly permissive entertaining and fun visiting relative figure rather than teacher or authority figure (Hetherington & Stanley-Hagen, 1997).

Investigations have consistently revealed that frequency of father–child contact has little correspondence to child adjustment. Moreover, though children who do feel close to their fathers are better adjusted, frequency of visitation has little relationship to these feelings (see the meta-analysis by Amato & Gilbreth, 1999). Evidence suggests that quality of contact is more important; when fathers are involved with homework, discipline, monitor activities, praise their children, and talk about school, children are better adjusted than those with more frequent but frivolous interaction (see Stewart, 2003).

Another obstacle to parental involvement is remarriage of either parent (Cooksey & Craig, 1998). With remarriage, and especially with the presence of new biological children or stepchildren, the roles of father and husband are once more psychologically completed, thus reducing the father's need for contact with his other children (Kissman, 1997). It also reduces the time, money, and availability of the father (Cooksey & Craig, 1998). The extent to which expectations of fatherhood itself become important, as opposed to a joint role of father and husband, the more fathers may continue active involvement in their children's lives (Kissman, 1997).

Nonresidential mothers are subject to role and identity issues as well (Kissman 1997). Many noncustodial mothers suffer almost unbearable guilt for relinquishing or not succeeding in attaining custody because of society's preference for maternal custody. This guilt can be intensified depending on the mother's immediate networks. Such guilt can have a debilitating effect that in turn affects mothers' ability to become involved with their children (Kissman, 1977).

There is little debate that, in theory, it is in a child's best interest for both parents to stay involved in the child's life. Children overwhelmingly experience a sense of loss when, due to divorce, contact with a nonresidential parent diminishes or is cut off (Wolchik et al., 1996). Research consistently reveals this is children's chief complaint about divorce (Kelly, 1993). However, the extent to which contact actually incurs benefits for children is under debate, as are custody arrangements.

Adverse effects for parental conflict between married parents on child adjustment and behavior are well documented (Grych & Fincham, 1990). There is no reason to suspect that conflict between divorced parents would be any less damaging to the child than conflict between married parents. Indeed, child adjustment seems to be better predicted by parental conflict than by family structure (Kot & Shoemaker, 1999). Amato and Rezac (1994) reviewed 33 studies that directly examined the hypothesis that frequency of contact with the nonresidential parent was positively correlated with the child's well-being. In all but one study the father was the nonresident parent. They found that 18 of the studies supported the hypothesis, 9 studies reported no association, and 6 studies found that the greater the contact from the nonresident parents, the greater the problems for the child. They recognized that some methodological or sample differences might explain some of these differences, yet they proposed that most of the effect was due to the relationship between the parents.

In situations of parental hostility, the child may actually fare better with decreased parental contact as increased contact with children generally involves increased contact and coordination among the divorced spouses. The potential benefits of nonresidential parental involvement are thus often negated by increased hostilities. Hostile interactions and legal battles between current or ex-spouses appear to be directly linked to poor psychological and emotional adjustment and behavior problems of children (Buchanan & Heiges, 2001; Furstenberg & Nord, 1985). Children report feeling caught in the middle between their parents (Afifi & Schrodt, 2003). Alternatively, sometimes when the parents are no longing living together promoting daily friction, the child and nonresident parent can actually become closer and more involved with each other (Hetherington, Cox, & Cox, 1982).

Undoubtedly, children desire unrestricted and flexible access to both parents (Neugebauer, 1989), and increasing paternal involvement in children's lives is precisely the reason joint legal custody is beginning to occur (Braver & O'Connell, 1998). Joint legal custody accounts for about 17% of custody arrangements, and joint physical custody accounts for about 7% (Nord & Zill, 1996). Evidence indicates that when such arrangements are exercised cooperatively, mother, father, and child are all better adjusted (Kelly, 2000). However, joint legal custody still does little to engage the nonresidential parent on a daily basis and is not necessarily beneficial. Arendell (1997) summarized research on joint custody and reported, "Probably the best conclusion that can be drawn from existing research is that joint custody appears to be preferable when both parents elect this option, but that joint custody should not be imposed on unwilling parents in mediation or in a court hearing" (p. 26).

Studies are starting to emerge that emphasize the perception of the father to the child, or the symbolic contact between father and child. When noncustodial parents take care to communicate the importance of their relationships with their children, this may help children adjust almost as much as continuing contact. Buchanan, Maccoby, and Dornbusch (1996) found that when noncustodial parents (mother or father) remember special days such as holidays and birthdays, children show better adjustment, even in the absence of frequent contact (Buchanan, 2000). Children's positive perceptions of bond with their nonresidential parent is a better predictor of their well-being than actual frequency of contact (Amato & Rezac, 1994).

Separation Due to Parental Incarceration

The fastest growing reason children are separated from a parent is incarceration (Brenner, 2001). The number of fathers in prison grew by 61% in the 1990s, and the number of imprisoned mothers grew by 85% (Mumola, 2000). In 1999, state and federal prisons held 721,500 parents of minor children. Approximately one third of fathers and just more than one half of mothers in state prisons report that at least one minor child lived with them at the time of their arrest (Mumola, 2000). About 2% of U.S. children have one or both parents incarcerated (Reed & Reed, 1997).

Little consensus exists as to the extent of the impact of parental incarceration on children. Research is scarce, and that which has been conducted is based on small samples, anecdotal evidence, and indirect methods of assessment (Seymour, 1998). Limited evidence appears to suggest that at least some children of incarcerated parents face many obstacles and have numerous emotional and behavioral problems (Seymour, 1998).

For children with close ties to a parent before imprisonment the separation is traumatic. Parental incarceration contributes to poor school work; alcohol and drug abuse problems (Arditti et al., 2003); and periods of denial, depression, sleeplessness, and anger (Brooks, 1993; Snyder, Carlo, & Coats, 2001). Children of an imprisoned parent often feel embarrassed and stigmatized (Gabel, 1992). In some cases, in efforts to protect them, children are not told the reason for their parent's absence and are left to make sense out of the situation (Gabel, 1992).

Families separated by incarceration also deal with role changes. Many incarcerated fathers lived in the same home with at least one of their children and contributed emotional support; sometimes they were the sole means of the child's financial report (Hairston, 2001a). The inability to provide for the family contributes to feeling unneeded and less connected (Fishman, 1990). Children of incarcerated parents have difficulty delineating roles; they often attempt to take over role responsibilities of the incarcerated parent (Brooks, 1993).

The question of child contact with incarcerated parents, especially visits in prison, is a hotly debated topic. The vast majority of imprisoned parents, fathers and mothers, have some sort of contact (e.g., letters) at least monthly with their children, yet approximately 55% of both mothers and fathers have never received an in-person visit from their children (Mumola, 2000). Visitation increases the likelihood of family reunification or, if the parents are no longer romantically involved, which is the vast majority (Mumola, 2000), continued parent–child relationships after release (Hairston, 2001a).

Visitation and other means of contact are frequently supported only in theory; actual institutional practices often impede rather than promote family ties. Institutional policies sometimes make family or child visits uncomfortable, difficult, or even degrading and humiliating (Hairston, 2001b). However, most fathers do not report prison regulations as the largest obstacle to seeing their children. Rather, they report a strained relationship with their children's mother impedes visitation. Children have no one to bring them (Hairston, 2001a).

Communication by phone, cards and letters, and visits, helps incarcerated members remain emotionally attached to children (Hairston, 2001a). Collect calls can be placed by prisoners but frequently they are significantly more costly than long-distance calls placed outside the prison (Hairston, 2001b). Most prisoners are offered the opportunity to write to their children. However, some states have restrictions on the number of letters that may be sent per month and most states mark letters from prison identifying them as such, adding to the embarrassment of the child receiving them (Hairston, 1998). Moreover, for some inmates and their families, the simple necessities to write letters, such as the cost of postage, are difficult to manage. Younger children are unlikely to have access to the supplies necessary nor the knowledge of how to post a letter, placing more dependence on adults for even this mode of contact.

Alternatively, some imprisoned parents do not want contact with their child, especially not FtF visits. Fear is expressed that the experience will be emotionally painful or damaging for the child. Sometimes the custodial parent or extended family networks also believe visitation would be detrimental for the child, as do many professionals within corrections and social services (Hairston, 2001b). Nonetheless, the limited evidence suggests that visitation facilitates child adjustment and parent–child bonds. However, given a deficit of large-scale longitudinal research and the wide range of circumstances, a blanket conclusion that increased contact facilitates child adjustment can not be reached; each situation must be considered on a case-by-case basis.

Imprisoned parents do think about their children, even with little interaction. Nurse (2002) interviewed several hundred fathers and found that many incarcerated men had daydreams about relationships with their children. These prisoners had high hopes and expectations. They looked forward to being called daddy and entertained thoughts of how their children would treat them with respect and affection. A difficult transition often ensues. One third of Nurse's respondents reported that their children did not recognize them and some called other individuals daddy, adding to the recently released father's disappointment. When the relationship between the father and the mother is weak or difficult, the father has limited access even after release, especially if he was not married to his child's mother. Obviously, the homecoming depends on the nature of the relationship with both the children and the children's primary caregiver, as well as the length of, and reason for, imprisonment.

CONCLUSIONS

The question, "What are the effects on the child of parental absence?" does not have a clear answer. The impact of the separation on the child seems to be dependent on the child's age, development, relationship between the child's parents, and a host of other complex and interrelated factors. As a general rule, the more influence and control children have over factors surrounding their circumstances during the separation, the better adjusted they tend to be (Ursano & Norwood, 1996). Children's adjustment, and family disruption overall, is in part contingent on reasons for separation. Parental absence due to socially acceptable reasons in general does not have the same ramifications as those that are socially stigmatized (Lowenstein, 1986).

The permanently nonresidential parent faces different obstacles in maintaining contact with children than does the temporarily separated parent. In the case of noncustodial parents, barriers may be more complex than geographical constraints. It is undeniable that positive, cooperative, consistent coparenting increases parental involvement with children and is in children's and parents' best interests. Yet, conflict-ridden involvement may be unhealthy. In addition, for many parents contact is often contingent on circumstances beyond their control. From the child's perspective, separation is almost always involuntary, although, as mentioned in chapter 7, some adolescents do voluntarily leave home either in search of means to support their families or to escape dysfunctional family environments.

In sum, though little is known about how to facilitate child well-being, less is known about sustaining close ties during the absence. Few concrete conclusions can be drawn aside from the fact that many children want involvement with both mothers and fathers, and quality of that involvement is more important than sheer frequency of contact. "Research indicates that the type of involvement matters. Father contact by itself generally is not associated with positive outcomes; the quality, such as affective closeness of the relationship and the type of parenting practices engaged in are" (King et al., 2004, p. 3). Yet most research continues to concentrate entirely on frequency of contact. Just as with dating partners and adult unions, when separated, communication that symbolizes and recognizes a relationship appears beneficial, regardless of reason for separation. Connections are facilitated through positive mental constructions of relationships in the absence of interaction.

Nonetheless, all separations are not the same. Single mothers, whether divorced, never married, or functionally single with an incarcerated partner, have the lowest household income per capita; a staggering number are below the poverty level (Arditti et al., 2003; Lamb, 1997). Poverty is not a factor among children separated from parents in dual-career families, and although income may be low among deployed military families, abject poverty is not usually an issue. Some children have cooperative co-parents acting in their best interests; some have parents who act more like children, neglecting the ramifications of their behavior on their children.

Children of dual-career professionals and military personnel may simultaneously miss their parents and feel proud of them; children of incarcerated parents often face shame. All parent–child separations clearly are not equal.

7

Across Generations:
Adult Children, Parents,
and Grandparents

Culturally, we are preoccupied with romantic and young child–parent relationships. This predilection is peculiar as these relationships are relatively short-lived across one's entire life span. Involuntary kinships are often more enduring than romantic relationships, and most individuals will spend more of their lifetime in relationships with parents and grandparents as adults than as young children (Bedford & Blieszner, 2000).

The connection across distances is considered in two spans of the child–parent relationship: the young adult–parent relationship and the middle-age child–older parent relationship. Admittedly, these two eras are arbitrary without clear demarcations, yet they serve as an organizational scheme. Attention then turns to grandparent–grandchild relationships. Relationships of elderly adults are then discussed. Meanings of success and cultural assumptions surrounding these intergenerational relations are offered first.

SUCCESS

As with most other relational research, success is ill defined, with different studies invoking different constructs such as feelings of attachment, closeness, intimacy, exchange, strain, parental dissatisfaction with adult children, and degree of conflict or disagreement. There is little agreement on what constitutes adult child–parent relational quality, much less on how to assess it (Lye, 1996). The same holds for relationships with grandparents.

Undoubtedly, what is deemed a satisfactory, or even acceptable, relationship differs among relational participants. For example, grandparents see their relationships with grandchildren as closer than do the grandchildren; adult grandchildren see their relationships with their grandparents as more active than do grandparents (Harwood, 2001).

If areas of study in the extant literature are used as indicators of success, success for young adults is, arguably, the healthy balance of independence and connection with parents. For the middle-aged child–parent relationship, the literature is preoccupied with the availability of children to care for elderly parents and the potential strain of caring for elderly parents while simultaneously parenting younger children, as the term the *sandwich* generation reflects (Williams & Nussbaum, 2001).

Successful grandparent–grandchild relationships are most often considered in terms of family solidarity. Individually, however, the quality of relationships with grandchildren seems to influence grandparents' overall psychological well-being. The grandchild may provide a sense of connection, an opportunity for social interaction, a sense of pride, and a feeling that the relationship "keeps them young" (Harwood, 2000a; Harwood & Lin, 2000; Harwood, McKee, & Lin, 2000).

The benefits are not one-sided. Like elderly parents, grandparents offer many unacknowledged contributions to family members. Grandchildren's emotional development and self-esteem appear to be linked to positive interaction with grandparents (Harwood, 2000b). They serve as role models for grandchildren, provide economic resources, and contribute to a sense of continuity (Bengston, 2001). For purposes here, success is considered continued affectionate ties, broadly construed.

CULTURAL ASSUMPTIONS

The stereotypical picture of this society as one of forlorn adults who are abandoned by their children and grandchildren is far from reality. Across all ages of parents and adult children, contact in one form or another is relatively frequent. Moreover, parent–child relationships are generally characterized by caring and closeness through the life span (Williams & Nussbaum, 2001).

Another myth is that older adults are ill and force themselves into their children's homes, becoming burdens to them (Hummert & Nussbaum, 2001). This is inaccurate on both counts. Coresidence is generally not preferred by either generation. In 1992 only about 15% of individuals over 65 resided with adult children. These numbers are slightly higher among African American and Hispanic populations than among White populations (Williams & Nussbaum, 2001). Less than 1 out of 3 of those who do co-reside do so for reasons related to the elderly parent's health. In fact, nearly two thirds of coresidential arrangements are because of the adult child's needs, such as housing following a divorce or unemployment (Treas & Lawton, 1999).

In addition to a preference for independent living, most elderly adults desire to avoid being a burden. In contrast, older adults often feel an obligation to provide resources to their adult children (Lye, 1996). Being a resource and not a liability to one's children appears to be an important component of self-definition. The view of oneself as parent, and thus provider and protector of one's children, remains salient regardless of age (Dunham, 1995).

Indeed, assistance is much more likely from parent to adult child than vice versa for many years. Though many elderly adults will require some type of care at some point, a deficit view of older adults disregards the many years that transpire during which older parents do not require such care; rather, they fulfill significant roles for family members. "Based on extensive research conducted over the past 30 years, family researchers have concluded that American adults and their parents are engaged in extensive and continuous exchanges of assistance, that most exchange is reciprocal, and that parents do not become net recipients of aid until they become very elderly or frail" (Lye, 1996, p. 84). Though not uniform, more often the flow or resources from parent to child continues through most of the life span. Parents often furnish a home, care for grandchildren, assist during illness or other crisis, give emotional support, or aid financially, though the exact nature of the support varies greatly by social class. Both intergenerational stake hypotheses and family solidarity perspectives have been used to explain such occurrences (see chap. 3, this volume).

Another prevalent assumption is that across all ages of adult children and parents, when distance increases, regular contact, emotionally close ties, and exchange of assistance are less likely (Treas & Lawton, 1999). In addition, feelings of obligation have been proposed to be weaker (Lye, 1996). However, most adult children live within 1 hour's drive of at least one parent, and about two thirds of elderly individuals with children live within 30 minutes of an adult child (Lye, 1996). Thus, concern about elderly adults lacking proximal kin is unfounded for most.

Moreover, even if proximity is linked to frequency of FtF visits and some types of support (e.g., instrumental tasks requiring physical access), distance has not consistently been found to be related to feelings of affective closeness (Kaufman & Uhlenberg, 1998). Perceptions of positive close connections are more important than physical distance for many types of support, both from parents to children and vice versa. Affective closeness is more predictive than distance for "important" conversations between adult child and parent as well (Dewit, Wister, & Burch, 1988; Treas & Lawton, 1999). In short, geographic distance does not pose an insurmountable obstacle to inter-generational relationships.

ADULT CHILD–PARENT RELATIONSHIPS

Young Adult–Parent Relationships

The number of young adults who reside with a parent or parents is difficult to establish. Although the Census Bureau reported that approximately 50% of individuals between the ages of 18 and 24 lived at home during 2002, this number includes single individuals living in college dorms. Similarly, research often does not count those living in college dorms or military barracks, as the family of origin's home is still considered the young adult's residence.

Although the retention of a parental home as an address may be psychologically meaningful to both parent and child, it ignores the reality that parent and child are not coresiding on a daily basis; thus, opportunities for FtF contact are, by default, lessened. Interaction is surely different among young adults residing full-time at a parental home versus those who report the family residence as their permanent residence but do not spend much of the year there.

Given that nearly one half of high school graduates attend college, the number of young adults actually residing with parents is much less than such estimates reflect. Even among those who do reside with one parent, many do not, and have not, lived with the other parent. Also, some adolescents live as emancipated minors, not residing with either parent and are functionally adults.

Though the paths to adulthood are diverse and ambiguous in U.S. society, two general adaptation periods are prevalent. The first is the establishment of psychological independence in adolescence, and the second, about 10 years later, is the establishment of practical independence; this includes moving away from the parental residence (Sherrod, 1996). Indeed, moving out of the parental home, whether to a residential college, down the street, or to a different town has been reported in one study of young adults to be the most important turning point in their relationships with their parents (Golish, 2000).

College has been characterized as a transitional phase, a haven for exploration, yet about one half the U.S. population does not attend college, and fewer complete college and thus do not have the luxury or the ambiguity of this gradual transition. Some young adults are not even afforded the gradual transition of high school. Estimates indicate that approximately 126,000 migrant farm workers in the United States are between ages 14 and 17; more than one half of these live away from their families, many of which are in Mexico, to find work and help support them (Gabbard, Mines, & Boccalandro, 1994; Huang, 2002).

Another instance of adolescents living apart from parents is "runaways" and "throwaways." Somewhere between .5 million and 1 million adolescents run away from home each year (Thompson, Kost, & Pollio, 2003). Although this departure has been thought of as rebellion, indications are that most leave to escape dysfunctional home environments of parental drug abuse or physical or sexual abuse. Throwaways are adolescents who are pushed out by uninterested parents (Whitbeck, Hoyt, & Ackley, 1997).

The juxtaposition of the conditions of the middle-class young adult college student living away from home with the teenage migrant worker or the unwanted and abused teenager is stark. These "adults" have little access to any type of school, health care, adult supervision, or even safe living conditions. The number of injuries and fatalities of the youth who engage in long hours of physically taxing farm labor is alarming and has prompted attention from the National Institute for Occupational Safety and Health (Vela & Lee, 2001). Supervision or guidance of any kind is often missing, though many do develop and travel in extensive fictive kinship networks. Allegiance to the family at home remains strong as evidenced by the flow of monetary resources from the adolescent back to family (Gabbard et al., 1994). Alternatively, runaways and throwaways attempt to distance themselves from parents and thus avoid agencies that could provide assistance out of concern they will be returned to their home environment. Different, but equally dangerous, risk factors are prevalent for these youth fending for themselves as adults in urban environments.

Relational Maintenance

Despite such varied arrangements and transitions to adulthood, the scant research that does exist on long-distance young adult–parent relationships has been conducted almost exclusively on college students and their parents. Attachment theory serves as the basis of many of those studies (see chap. 3, this volume). The premise is that young college students with close emotional bonds stay in touch with parents who serve as a secure base for exploration. Students with emotionally close ties to their parents have been found to make more frequent phone calls, write more letters, have more FtF visits, and exchange more e-mail than those with less close ties. In addition, emotionally close students increase contact during times of stress, thus supporting an attachment paradigm (Kenny & Donaldson, 1991; Lapsley, Rice, & Fitzgerald, 1990; Trice, 2002).

Trice (2002) pointed out that studies before the widespread use of e-mail showed an average of two contacts per week between parents and college freshmen (e.g., Dubas & Peterson, 1996), whereas students in her study tripled the number of contacts per week through e-mail alone. Though not examined, Trice raised a concern that this level of contact may not be conducive to fostering independence; e-mail has made contact too available. Despite such concerns, in general, frequency of contact through phone, letter, or personal visits is associated with young adults' feelings of closeness with parents and with satisfaction with the parent–child relationship, but not with the young adults' adjustment or lack thereof (Dubas & Peterson, 1996).

Overall, distance is associated with a decline of contact between young adult children and parents as well as less assistance from children to their parents, as this help is generally instrumental. However, distance does not seem to be related to parental help to their young adult children as this help is most often financial or in the giving of advice (Rossi & Rossi, 1990). Of course this ignores the reality of some young adults who do not attend college and live away from home precisely to provide monetary resources to their families.

Even if proximity, contact, and feelings of closeness do correlate, the nature of these interrelationships is unknown. Distance may reflect other dynamics: Young adults who do not desire contact, and who are not emotionally close, may opt to live farther away (Silverstein, Lawton, & Bengston, 1994).

Others, also from an attachment theory perspective, have argued that neither distance nor lessened contact is particularly detrimental. Amato and Rezac (1994) found that the length of time since the last contact between young adults and their parents was not related to the importance these young adults placed on their relationships with their parents. "As adult children move from the home and increase the physical as well as psychological distance from their parents, the mechanism of symbolic attachment emerges" (Williams & Nussbaum, 2001, p. 155). Young adults draw on imagined or symbolic representations of their parents. They play out conversations with parents mentally resulting in feelings of closeness and security (Cicirelli, 1991). When such cognitions and memories are combined with some mediated communication, both the adult child and the parent are able to maintain a sense of secure attachment and closeness. This means of relational maintenance has been proposed to continue throughout all ages of adulthood. Physical proximity then is not seen as a deterrent to feelings of closeness or affective ties.

Extremely Proximal Young Adult–Parent Relationships

If one endorses the prevailing assumption that proximity and frequency of interaction promote relational closeness, then adult children and parents who live together should have the closest relationships. This logic does not hold. Coresidence may not promote healthy parent–adult child relationships and has even been said to demonstrate less than optimal adjustment on the part of the adult child (Dubas & Peterson, 1996).

Neither position is absolute. Rather, expectations play a large role in the quality of relationships between adult children living at home and parents. In earlier eras, coresidence until marriage was normative (White, 1994). Today, both parents and children have global expectations that a child will live away from the parents without marriage (Graber & Brooks-Gunn, 1996). Either staying too long or leaving too soon may be considered off-time and thus create tension in the relationship. What is off-time is contingent on numerous individual parent and child characteristics, family norms, and circumstances surrounding the coresidence that are beyond the current scope (see White, 1994). Overall, to promote positive relationships, a young adult's continued residence or return to a parental home is best viewed as a "temporary, and orderly way to prepare for adulthood, not an indulgence of insecurity or irresponsibility" (Fulmer, 1999, p. 216). White (1994) has identified family metaphors for the parental home. The metaphors of home as a safety net, implying failure, versus a home base, implying a normative gradual departure, are telling of the differing parental expectations for departure.

Perhaps too much emphasis has been placed on the separation of the adult child from the parents, and too little on connectedness. If indeed this period is one of separation, and as some have proposed, even necessary separation resulting in temporary estrangement from parents, the study of the process of renegotiation of connection after the establishment of independence is needed (Cooney, 1997). The question that is beginning to be asked is, "How does one establish oneself as an independent, self-reliant adult while at the same time maintaining close familial ties?" (Dubas & Peterson, 1996, p. 4).

Middle-Aged Children and Parents

Whereas autonomy is a predominant issue during the young adult years, the availability of the middle-aged child to provide support to the elderly parent has been at the center of much research during the older parent years. Adult children are the most common caregivers for older adults, more so than spouses, other kin, or friends and neighbors (Lin & Rogerson, 1995). Concerns about the availability of children to care for adults have increased because of increased life expectancy and the decrease in fertility rates. In other words, people will be elderly longer, with fewer children for assistance (Lin & Rogerson, 1995).

Research focus has been on the determinants of proximity, as proximity has been considered to be a primary factor in the type and frequency of interaction between adult children and their parents (Lin & Rogerson, 1995; Williams & Nussbaum, 2001). The concern here, however, is not with what determines proximity but rather how relationships are enacted when the relational participants are not geographically close.

There is little question that geographic proximity influences interaction between adult children and parents. Comprehensive reviews have revealed that for both White and Black elderly populations in the United States, the geographic distance is the strongest predictor of frequency of interaction between adult children and their parents, even after controlling for age, sex, marital status, length of residence, and income (Dewit et al., 1988; Smith, 1998). In close proximity, FtF contact occurs frequently. When distance goes beyond a one-half day drive, frequent FtF contact becomes replaced by less frequent visits overall and more overnight visits, letter writing, and telephone conversations (Dewitt, et al., 1988).

Geographically distant parent–adult child relationships are not inherently less strong than those that are proximal (Baldock, 2000). Unequivocally, distance does limit certain types of interaction; instrumental tasks that must be performed daily can not be completed from a distance. However, emotional support can be readily given over the phone regardless of distance (Litwak, 1985). Close relationships between middle-aged adults and parents have been found to be maintained through letters and telephone calls (Baldock, 2000).

Although the preferred societal model is that needs of aging parents should be met by their children, such provision may put adults at risk for depression, as they begin to fear becoming more and more dependent on their children (Dunham, 1995). Moreover, proximity increases opportunities for conflict, and several studies have found that conflict between adult children and parents or problems in the life of the adult child providing care can lead to lower life satisfaction among parents (Dunham, 1995). Similarly, coresidence or extreme proximity have been related to dissatisfaction about the relationship, struggles for independence, and conflict between older adults and their children (Luescher & Pillemer, 1998). Moreover, frequency of FtF interaction does not necessarily translate into more positive relationships. Given the potential primordial attachment between parent and child, "the relationship may be actively maintained over long periods of discomfort and stress" (Silverstein et al., 1994, p. 67).

Though principal interest has been in the availability of adult children to provide care, another significant area of research has been the strain of providing this care on the children (Williams & Nussbaum, 2001). However, the stress of the adult child, who is geographically separated, is often overlooked. Middle-aged children living away from their parents report worry and anguish as parents age and health concerns become more salient (Baldock, 2000; Cimo, 1992).

Such anxiety is of particular interest among military personnel as "active duty military represents one of the largest groups of people who live long distances from their parents for most of their adult lives and have restricted opportunities to visit parents" (Parker, Vaughn, Dunkle, & Vaitkus, 2002, p. 259). At mid-career, 84% of officers have at least one parent alive, and a substantial proportion of these express worry over their parent's health (Parker, et al., 2002).

Overseas deployments escalate these anxieties. Guilt and feelings of inadequacy are also factors for these individuals, as they live in contradiction to beliefs and expectations about providing proximal care for their elderly parents. As discussed in chapter 5, the military has a vested interest in assisting in these situations, as family stressors often interfere with duties. Parker et al. (2002) found that among senior officers, telephone, e-mail, or letter contact occurs weekly. Increased telephone and mail contact serves to monitor their parents' health and cope with their own concerns about their parents.

In sum, research has taken a problem-oriented approach to aging and adult children's relationships with their elderly parents. Yet, research is beginning to be directed toward strengths and resilience in aging well and the reciprocal support elderly provide for other family members (Allen, Blieszner, & Roberto, 2000). More work is needed on noncrisis connections (Cooney, 1997), as these predominate for many years and constitute relationships on a daily basis.

CONCLUSIONS

Relationships among adult children and their parents at all ages are characterized by conflicting societal expectations of obligation and independence (Aldous, 1995). The first is that parents and children have a life-long obligation to care for and assist each other. The second is that adults are responsible for their own well-being. "Relations between adult children and their parents represent a delicate balance of these two norms" (Lye, 1996, p. 95).

Research interest is almost exclusively in the development of the young adult child, with parent–child relationships only of interest insofar as they influence this development. When the relationship between young adults and their parents is examined, most research has looked at either the effect of life-course transitions, such as child marriage or parental divorce on the relationship, or to a lesser extent the effect of parent–adult child relationship on the well-being of both (Knoester, 2003). Little research has directly examined "the mechanisms through which their lives remain linked" (Knoester, 2003, p. 1433).

GRANDPARENT–GRANDCHILD RELATIONSHIPS

Estimates project that 75% of the population will be a grandparent. In addition, the sheer number of years individuals will spend as a grandparent is greater than previous generations (Bengston, 2001). In 2002, approximately 31% of adults were grandparents and 8% of all children under age 18 lived with at least one grandparent (Fields, 2003). In just more than one half of these cases, a parent was not present: The grandparent was the primary caregiver. Of course, even in these households, the grandparent is likely to have other grandchildren with whom they do not reside.

Cultural Assumptions

Positive societal images are projected onto the grandparenting role (Williams & Nussbaum, 2001). Beyond this generalization, scholars disagree on the extent to which norms about the role of grandparent exist in the United States. Some have attempted categorization of grandparenting types (see Williams & Nussbaum, 2001, for a review). Others have argued that the role of grandparent as currently conceived in U.S. culture is "tenuous and ambiguous, with few normative expectations" (Mills, 2001, p. 403).

The role of grandparent is diverse, dynamic, and complex. Roles change as the age of the grandchild and the grandparent change: "Grandparents range in age from 30 to 110, and their grandchildren are infants as well as retirees" (Spence, Black, Adams, & Crowther, 2001, p. 524). Roles may change with the divorce or remarriage of the adult children; grandparents may find themselves as the primary caregiver of their grandchild or negotiating joint care giving with a parent. Roles also may change with their own divorce or remarriage. Individuals may become first-time grandparents or have additional grandchildren because of their own, or their children's, remarriage (Mills, 2001). These grandparent–grandchild relationships often begin with the grandchild as an adolescent or adult. The already ambiguous nature of the role of grandparent is amplified.

Relational Maintenance

A host of factors have relational ramifications for the grandparent–grandchild relationships. Three factors, though, may be especially influential. These are acceptance of a grandparent role, the relationship between the grandparent and parent, and geographic proximity. Each of these is briefly discussed in turn.

For a positive grandparent–grandchild relationship, the grandparent must accept the role. The advent of the first grandchild is "a significant symbolic marker of advancing age, which is not seen so positively in our culture" (Williams & Nussbaum, 2001, p. 173). When individuals feel they are too young to be grandparents, or that their child is too young to be a parent, the event is seen as off-time. This may influence grandparents' desire for the relationship.

Timing can also create tension between the grandparent and the parent (Harwood, 2001). The relationship between the grandparent and parent is the most pivotal factor in grandparent–grandchild relationships, as young children's opportunities for interaction with grandparents are mediated by parents (Downs, 1989; Holladay et al., 1997). Thus, a strained relationship between a parent and grandparent impede the grandparent–grandchild relationship. In the event of parental divorce, the paternal grandparents' ties are generally weakened as the mother generally has custody (Bengston, 2001). The custodial parent may block access to the ex-spouses' parents (Cherlin & Furstenberg, 1985), though visitation rights of grandparents are currently being debated in the courts.

Even among college students, most contact between grandparents and grandchildren takes place in the presence of the middle generation, often in conjunction with family events (Harwood, 2000b). As children move into young adulthood, their relationship with grandparents may be more voluntary than obligatory, as parental gatekeeping lessens (Holladay et al., 1997). For example, though parental divorce may have a tremendous impact on the grandparent–grandchild relationship when the child is young, when divorce occurs after the grandchild is a young adult, it appears to have little effect on the relationship (see Williams & Nussbaum, 2001).

Turning directly to proximity, "a new study is not needed to establish that geographic distance is a strong predictor of frequency of intergenerational contact. Every study that includes a measure of distance finds that the closer grandparents live to their grandchildren, the more likely they are to visit frequently" (Uhlenberg & Hammill, 1998, p. 276). In addition, grandparents who live nearby their young grandchildren tend to be involved on a routine basis (Cherlin & Furstenberg, 1985), and grandparents and grandchildren who do not live close together express frustration with limited opportunities to interact (Downs, 1989).

College-age grandchildren report that emotional closeness and affection for grandparents remain high in the college years (Creasey & Kaliher, 1994). Even from a distance, college students see their grandparents as more accepting of open conversations than parents. A grandparent is often seen as a confidant and more understanding than a parent. Grandchildren also look to grandparents as role models, and family histories are learned from grandparents, as is the value and importance of family (Harwood et al., 2000; Nussbaum & Bettini, 1994).

Limited research has provided some indication of the qualities of interaction that seem to co-occur with positive relationships. College-age "grandchildren and grandparents who perceived their partners as complimenting them, showing affection, showing respect, sharing personal thoughts and feelings, being attentive, and being supportive were consistently more content and involved in their relationships" (Harwood, 2000b, p. 759). Perceptions of mutual involvement, kindness, self-disclosure, support and grandparents' storytelling have been related to solidarity (Harwood, 2001). As most contact has been initiated by parents, from the grandparents' perspective, contact initiated by the young adult is especially meaningful (Harwood & Lin, 2000).

Even if grandparents and grandchildren resided in geographic proximity during the grandchild's childhood, the probability of geographic proximity with a young adult grandchild is certainly much less. Given this, mediated communication becomes especially important (Harwood, 2000a,). When including any type of media, Harwood (2000a) found that 62% of his college student sample communicated in some manner with a grandparent at least a few times each month. Though frequency of contact may well be associated with geographic distance, "frequency of contact alone cannot be used to infer the quality of ties between grandchildren and their elders" (Boon & Brussoni, 1996, p. 444). There appears to be virtually no correlation between proximity and feelings of closeness or personal involvement in college student–grandparent relationships (Boon & Brussoni, 1996; Harwood, 2000a). Harwood proposed that feelings of closeness are probably established by this time and thus less susceptible to geographic distance.

E-mail is becoming a viable mode of correspondence between young adults and their grandparents; use of the Internet among seniors jumped by 47% between 2000 and 2004 (Internet & American Life Project, 2004a). Drawing on media richness theory, Harwood (2000a) argued that e-mail may be ideally suited for college grandparent–grandchild relationships as the fact that communication occurs may be the most important aspect of the interaction for these relationships. Low-richness media (e.g., e-mail) may be ideal for situations with ambiguous roles wherein relationships must be negotiated. This is precisely what grandparents and grandchildren are involved in during the college years.

The aforementioned research appears to operate on the presumption that the grandchild and grandparent had close ties when the child was young, and thus concern is with continuing those ties into adulthood. Yet questions about how solidarity or affection is achieved initially between grandparents and grandchildren who live significant distances apart remain unaddressed.

RELATIONSHIPS OF THE ELDERLY

Family relationships become more salient among the elderly as other networks, including spouses, have passed away (Bedford & Bleiszner, 2000). For many, the family exists in memory (Johnson, 2000). Family relationships may be almost totally sentimental or commemorative ones with little, if any, contact. Among elderly family members interaction is often intermittent in the form of letters and telephone calls, especially as difficulty with geographic mobility increases. Evidence supports the position that the amount or frequency of interaction among family members is not directly associated with the satisfaction or quality of the relationship or the meanings attached to those relationships (Johnson, 2000). Based on Johnson's (2000) work, Bedford and Blieszner (2000) asked, "Then under what circumstances does contact (or its lack) either enhance or interfere with satisfying family relationships in later life?" (p. 165).

Speculation has been offered that when the relationship was strained or conflictual in previous years, absence allows tensions to be managed and positive perceptions to be entertained. If contact then ensues, the difficulties in the relationship resurface (Bedford & Blieszner, 2000). Moreover, with no information to the contrary, one can assume a lack of contact from geographically distant relatives or friends is due to health or financial reasons rather than voluntary absence. When visits occur, the older family member sometimes attributes negative intentions to the visitor. "Lack of contact, thus, can potentiate the idealization of family relationships" (Bedford & Blieszner, 2000, p. 165).

Such ideas are not offered to legitimize a failure to maintain active engagement with elderly individuals, as positive contact clearly contributes to the well-being of elderly individuals, but rather both to question the assumption that mere interaction is necessarily positive and to point out another instance in which affectionate bonds are maintained through idealized memories.

CONCLUSIONS

This chapter has discussed dyads: young adult children and middle-aged parents, middle-aged children and elderly parents, and grandparents and grandchildren. Though a relationship may be dyadic, it occurs in and is influenced by the family as a whole and by complex cultural and family systems (Williams & Nussbaum, 2001). For example, the young adult's departure from the home sends reverberations through the entire system. Nonetheless, we know little beyond the dyadic level.

An additional problem is the absence of research on noncollege student young adult–parent relationships. As many college-age young adults do not attend college as do attend; these parent–young adult child relationships yield another understudied form. Moreover, the priority on identity development and individuality comes primarily from research on White middle-class samples of college students; this preoccupation with separation is not shared among all co-cultural groups (Cooney, 2000). To understand relationships among young adults and their parents, research must include more diverse populations.

Other limiting views include the myopic focus on two-parent, four-grandparent families. Children sometimes have persons other than a parent as their primary caregiver; they may have one parent, not two, or may have many sets of parents through remarriages and cohabitating arrangements. Grandchildren may have multiple configurations of grandparents, and grandparents may have multiple configurations of grandchildren. These complex kinships are primarily nonvoluntary, persistent, take place within a context of other relationships that span multiple generations and households, and are often "primarily sentimental or symbolic, in the absence of much FtF contact" (Bedford & Blieszner, 2000, p. 161). This absence of frequent FtF contact makes them no less meaningful and, pending the circumstances, sometimes more satisfactory than proximal relationships.

8

Peer Relationships: Siblings and Friends

$\mathcal{S}$iblings and friends may be in our lives for an incredible length of time. Siblings "may know each other years before meeting a spouse, and years after the death of their parent. Though one might spend forty to fifty years with one's parents, life with a sibling can last sixty to eighty years" (Bank & Kahn, 1997, p. 13). Similarly, long-term friends usually outlive our parents and often outlast our romantic involvements. Both relationships are vital for meeting various instrumental or emotional needs related to life satisfaction and successful aging (Hummert & Nussbaum, 2001). These two relationships, one generally considered obligatory and the other voluntary, are actually similar in many ways, including the manner in which they are maintained.

SIBLINGS

Across races and socioeconomic status most adults over age 55 have at least one living sibling; the average is 2.39 (Sweet, Bumpass, & Call, 1988). Just less than 50% of adults' siblings live more than 25 miles apart. Less than 25% live within 2 miles (Sweet et al., 1988). Though these numbers vary with race and socioeconomic status, obviously adult siblings do not predominantly live next door to each other or even in the same neighborhood. Nevertheless, proximity has been touted as a necessity for healthy sibling relationships in later life (e.g., Rosenberg & Anspach, 1973). Proximity has even served as the operationalization of relational closeness in some research: "Geographic proximity is included as a measure of the strength of the sibling tie" (White, 2001, p. 260; see also Bengston & Roberts, 1991). Sheer amount of interaction is also used as an index of closeness: "As indicated by frequency of contact, ties to full siblings are closer to those than to half or step brothers or sisters" (Treas & Lawton, 1999, p. 433).

Clearly, contact is not always FtF, and is not isomorphic with feelings of relational closeness. Nor is distance. Despite distance, most people in later life maintain some sort of contact with their siblings (see Cicirelli, 1996). They also feel close to each other (Cicirelli & Nussbaum, 1999). A large national study of various ages and races of adult siblings found that approximately one half of siblings see each other minimally once a month and nearly two thirds said a sibling was one of their closest friends (White & Riedmann, 1992a).

To consider maintaining long-distance sibling relationships, assumptions surrounding siblings are supplied and successful sibling ties considered. Attention then turns directly to proximity and maintenance.

Cultural Assumptions and Success

Claims about the importance of siblings presume siblings have a long history of shared early experiences and a strong sense of family forged from biological and residential connections (Cicirelli, Coward, & Dwyer, 1992). Siblings are said to be unique from other relational forms (Cicirelli, 1995; Cicirelli & Nussbaum, 1989). Full siblings share a gene pool, with 33% to 66% of their genes in common (Scarr & Gracek, 1992). This genetic link may account for some similarities in certain talents, abilities, or even medical conditions (Treas & Lawton, 1999). Second, siblings are more equal in power than any other close kin relationships. Also, the sheer longevity of the relationship also separates many sibling relationships from other relationships. For many individuals, sibships are their "longest enduring emotional bond" (Bedford, 1996, p. 123). Finally, it is assumed that siblings have an intimacy from sharing childhood experiences that cannot be easily replicated by others.

Clearly, such assumptions exclude numerous configurations of sibling relationships and reflect nucleocentric and genetic biases. Many siblings do not have two biological parents in common. Sibling relationships may be formed because of adoption. Siblings may be part or half (sharing one biological parent), step (because of the marriage or remarriage of one biological parent), quasi (children of different biological parents who are nonmarital cohabiters), foster, or fictive or surrogate (individuals who might or might not have legal or biological ties, such as cousins, but are functionally siblings). Siblings may be some combination of the preceding and likely many other arrangements. These relationships are situated in broader family contexts that impinge on them as well.

Assumptions of longevity, equality, and coresidential relationships are also problematic. Individuals may become siblings in later childhood or even adulthood because of the marital status of their parents. Some sibling relationships may be more egalitarian than many other relational forms, yet siblings may be spaced many years apart, contributing to power differentials.

Coresidence also cannot be assumed; the more years between siblings, the fewer coresidential years. In addition, some children's sibling relationships, whether full, half, step, or other, occur across households (Brannen, Heptinstall, & Bhopal, 2000). Full, step, or quasi siblings may live in different households all of the time or part of the time as children because of custody or foster care arrangements. Whether sibships are formed later in life or occur across residences, shared childhood experiences are not necessarily a given component of sibships. Even continued existence cannot be automatically assumed; stepsibling relationships technically cease to exist if their parents divorce. Yet, some of these same siblings may still consider themselves as such, whereas others may not. Nonetheless, siblings sharing two married residential biological parents are the societal standard by which other siblings are judged (Cicirelli, 1995).

Though it has been argued that siblings tend to provide more instrumental support, less emotional support, and less affectionate closeness than friendships (Bedford, 1996), this does not seem to hold throughout the life span. Somewhere at the margins of young adulthood and middle age and continuing through old age, sibling relationships become increasingly important. The literature on sibling relationships in adulthood, emphasizes feelings of attachment, positive affect (or affectionate closeness), and willingness to mobilize in times of need. These attributes, then, characterize successful adult-sibling relationships.

Maintaining Sibling Relationships

Despite the relative prominence, permanence, and potential importance of sibships, little work on the maintenance of sibling ties, at any age, has been conducted, though factors that influence contact in general have been identified. These include ethnicity, other relationships, sex of siblings, family size, and the strongest predictor, geographic closeness (Mares, 1995). Distance is usually considered only to the extent that it hinders interaction. Much like research on adult children and their parents, the central concern with proximity is with availability of siblings in times of need.

Sibling interaction and closeness decline in early adulthood, remain dormant during middle age, and resurface as prominent during older adulthood, remaining so through old age (Cicirelli, 1995). However, whether amount or frequency of contact increases or decreases with age and distance depends on what researchers count as interaction. When only FtF interaction is considered, contact declines. Seeing each other in person decreases as mobility problems increase, especially as distance increases, but if one considers telephone and letters, contact appears to increase in old age (Cicirelli, 1995).

One study explicitly examined maintenance activities of college students and their siblings who ranged in age from 12 to 89 years old (Meyers, 2001). Whether or not the siblings coresided or lived within geographic proximity was not reported. It is probably safe to assume that most did not reside together. Performing tasks was reported as a predominant means of relational mainte-nance among these siblings and was associated with liking each other. How-ever, the nature of these tasks was not reported. Being positive and reassuring was also associated with liking one's siblings. Little openness was found among these siblings and the proposal was offered that "openness is not essential to maintaining the sibling bond" (Meyers, 2001, p. 27).

In young adulthood, siblings seem to talk more about a wider variety of topics and do more activities with friends than with each other. Relationships with peers may be more important, at least in the daily lives of young adults (Pulakos, 1989). Some reports indicate increased negative feelings among siblings during young adulthood. Sibships have been characterized by rivalry and jealousy in arenas such as education or careers (Bedford, 1996). However, unless extreme, this negative involvement can co-occur with feelings of closeness (Cicirelli & Nussbaum, 1989).

During middle age, sibling relationships may fall into a dormant period as ca-reers and children take priority (Bank & Kahn, 1997). Nonetheless, siblings ex-press guilt, sadness, or anger about their lack of involvement in each others' lives (Bedford, 1996). Unlike parent–child relationships, few siblings rely on each other for tangible or instrumental help, but they do depend on each other for psycho-logical or emotional support and response in times of crisis (Cicirelli, 1995).

Indeed, a near universal of full sibships is that they may be activated in re-sponse to a crisis due to their obligatory component (Allan, 1977). Concern has been expressed about nonfull siblings' propensity to respond to each other's needs. The connection among siblings in adulthood is based on obligation and the attachments formed in early childhood interaction (Cicirelli, 1995). Step or half siblings may not have or feel the same obligation and may not have been provided the opportunity for attachments to form. Of course, full siblings do not always have this opportunity either.

As siblings move through middle age into older adulthood, they provide in-creased psychosocial support (Cicirelli, 1995). Feelings of rivalry continue to decline, though conflict can be substantive. Elderly siblings may "take precau-tion to avoid known sources of sibling conflict to assure that their interactions will be satisfying" (Bedford, 1996, p. 134).

Siblings may initiate contact in old age for various types of support; the ability to provide support for aging siblings of course depends on the health and circumstances of the other sibling. As with elderly parents and adult children, living nearby may be necessary for certain types of instrumental support, though proximity is not necessary for emotional support (Miner & Uhlenberg, 1997).

Age is not the only influence on relationships; a life-course perspective examines life events that influence sibling relationship (Cantor, 1979). For example, across races, ages, and socioeconomic status siblings tend to interact more frequently and rely on each other more following a divorce. The pattern is reversed with the arrival of children or a new marriage (White, 2001).

Care of elderly parents may require siblings to interact. The demands of caring for an adult parent do not necessarily reestablish positive relationships among siblings. Unresolved issues may reemerge (Bedford, 1996). Close to one half of adults caring for elderly parents report serious conflict with a sibling. Feelings of hostility or inequity may ensue between siblings who do not feel the other is doing his or her part (Strawbridge & Wallhagen, 1991).

Another crucial point is after the death of the last parent. As much contact has been orchestrated by parents (White, 2001), when parents die, sibling interaction generally decreases (Bedford, 1996). The relationship may become more voluntary than obligatory and siblings may find themselves having to think about maintaining their sibling ties (Vogl-Bauer, 2003).

Limited research reveals that individuals maintain step, half, and full sibships into adulthood but grant priority to full siblings over other forms (White & Riedmann, 1992b, p. 206). Full adult siblings see each other on the average two to three times a month and half siblings two to three times a year. The adult relationship between half siblings and stepsiblings appears to be highly contingent on the number of years of shared residence as children; contact is also more likely when the adults have fewer full siblings (White & Riedmann, 1992b). Given the decreasing number of full sibships, and growing configurations of other sibling relationships, it remains to be seen if sibships will become more voluntary or if stepsiblings' and half siblings' roles will become more obligatory.

Frequency of contact aside, findings are consistent that positive affect toward siblings increases with age. These positive perceptions of siblings may occur through "perceptual distortion and selection" to meet one's own needs (Bedford, 1996, p. 134). Thus, the role of positively biased mental constructions in maintaining relationships across time and distance again emerges.

"To explain the maintenance of the sibling bond over extended separations in space and time that occur in adulthood, we have argued that the propensity for closeness and contact with the attached figure (the sibling) continues through life but is satisfied on a symbolic level" (Cicirelli & Nussbaum, 1989, p. 289). This symbolic attachment is essential for an affective bond, though it may be supplemented by other means of direct contact. From this perspective, proximity is, in many ways, irrelevant to the nature of the relationship. Many interactions take place in thought (Bedford, 1996). Positive affect later in life appears to increase, regardless of contact (Cicirelli, 1995). Thirty years of cohort studies verify this (Bedford, 1996). Sibling relationships are "elusive, emotionally charged, memory-laden" bonds (Bedford, 1996, p. 134).

Summary

Obligation may be a greater motivation for contact among siblings than among other relational forms. Siblings engage in few social activities and discuss few topics, especially during young adulthood. Sibships may be successfully maintained for years with little direct contact. Contact may occur often more in thought than through FtF or mediated means. The simple thought of having a sibling is comforting for many elderly individuals. Individuals "gain a great sense of support from knowing that siblings were ready to give aid in time of trouble, although the help might be called for only on rare occasions" (Cicirelli & Nussbaum, 1989, p. 294). Contact aside, people with living siblings have higher morale in later life (McGhee, 1985).

The lack of research on maintenance of sibling relationships may be due to the emphasis on the nonvoluntary aspect of sibling relationships; they are simply supposed to be in a state of maintenance. They are continuous relationships, no matter how inactive. Sibling relationships can be reactivated on a moment's notice (Allan, 1977). "It is a relationship that most people maintain and nurture—or in some cases, perhaps, just endure—thru the entire lifespan and which, in old age, gains increasing prominence" (White, 2001, p. 567). Though U.S. culture touts frequent FtF interaction as a relational necessity, sibling relationships are maintained in the absence this interaction, through mediated means, through third parties such as parents, through symbolic representations, through memories, or through societal structures.

Though often considered obligatory, some have argued that sibling relationships have discretionary components. A more encompassing stance is that sibling relationships in some way resemble voluntary friendships; in other ways they may resemble obligatory parent–child relationships (Bedford, 1996; Cicirelli, 1996).

FRIENDSHIPS

Little agreement among scholars exists when it comes to defining friendship. Volumes have been written on the meaning of friendship and its roles or functions, levels, or types (see Fehr, 1996; Wright, 1984). Nussbaum (1994) described these prominent features of friendships. They are largely voluntary with no institutionalized recognition; they exist in the absence of blood or legal ties, and rituals to commemorate or formalize them are relatively rare in current U.S. culture, though friendship rituals do occur in some co-cultural groups. Friendships are egalitarian in that one friend has no authority over another. Friends generally provide support for each other freely, whereas obligations may drive other relationships. Nevertheless, expectations and norms for a particular friendship do develop across time. Friendships are a life-span phenomenon in that they may begin at any age and may be brief or long term (Nussbaum, 1994, pp. 211–212). Friends may be casual acquaintances or deeply intimate, trusted, committed, companions, though there are not generally agreed-on demarcations for various levels of friendship (Nussbaum, 1994).

The importance of a wide range of levels of friendships for our well-being cannot be overstated. Nonetheless, the literature prioritizes best friends and closeness, despite disagreement on what either concept means and the significance of other friendships. Closeness of best friends appears to be the implicitly invoked criteria for a successful friendship, at least in studies concerned with proximity.

Cultural Assumptions and Relational Maintenance

Three assumptions constrain views of long-distance friendships. First, long-distance friendships have been argued to exist rarely (Allan, 1979). Second, FtF interaction is, again, considered the best method for sustaining a friendship. Thus, long-distance friendships are inherently at risk (Davis, 1973). Third, if indeed long-distance friendships do occur, these friendships are seen as inherently less close; friends who do not spend a lot of time together simply cannot be as close as those who do (Berscheid et al., 1989). In short, long-distance friendships rarely exist and obviously cannot be as "close" as proximal friendships simply because the of the FtF time. These intertwined presumptions are examined in conjunction with relational maintenance.

The notion that long-distance friendships simply seldom occur has been successfully challenged. In a probability sampling of older adults in North Carolina, 40% of the sample had "emotionally close" friends who lived outside of the South (Adams & Blieszner, 1993). Other estimates place the number even higher, with 90% reporting at least one close long-distance friend (Rohfling, 1995).

The second assumption has two components; interactions should be FtF and they should be frequent. Neither component is central to friendships. Frequent interaction, in person, appears to be important for friendships among young children and this may hold, to some extent, throughout adolescence (Crosnoe, 2000). Using a social exchange approach (see chap. 3, this volume), Oswald and Clark (2003) hypothesized that long-distance friendships would be more costly in terms of investments and thus be more susceptible to deterioration. Contrary to this, they found proximity was not related to investment. Frequency of FtF interaction seems irrelevant to maintaining close friendships among young adults, though frequency of interaction of some kind, for example, by telephone is associated with best friend status (Oswald & Clark, 2003).

Studies of college students found no differences in the perception of closeness among proximal or long-distance friendships but did find the nature of contact to differ. Proximal friends engaged in more activities together and shared more common social contacts, but they were no more open or reassuring than distant friends. Long-distance college friends were also found to rely more on cards, letters, and phone calls to maintain their relationships than geographically close friends (Johnson, 2001). From these findings, the speculation is offered that individuals have different expectations for their long-distance friends, and frequent FtF contact simply is not one of them (Johnson, 2001).

As people age, it is more likely that some friends will not live nearby. When young, separations might cause a friendship to deteriorate (Nussbaum, 1994). Both for undergraduate college students and graduate students, friendships are more "self maintaining, more dependent on affection, less vulnerable to a decrease in contact than close friendships" among high school students (Rose & Serefica, 1986, p. 285).

A series of studies of middle-aged women confirm this trend (see Rohfling, 1995). These studies found that the women did not communicate frequently, either in person or through other means. Telephone calls were only occasional; nonetheless, they were the most frequent mode of contact. Other research on both sexes has found that when FtF encounters did take place, they more often occurred because one was going to be in vicinity of their friend for some other reason rather than a trip simply to see the friend (Adams & Blieszner, 1993; Rohfling, 1995). Yet these latent friendships are psychologically important (Adams, 1998).

Perhaps the lack of a need for physical presence for successful relationships is best seen among elderly adults. Among the elderly, friendship transcends interaction (Nussbaum, 1994). "With older adults, a relationship that is meaningful and rewarding is not dependent upon overt behavioral interaction, but can be maintained as a normal extension when friends physically move apart" (Nussbaum, 1994, p. 222). Friends separated by distance may be maintained in thought, as well as letter writing or visiting. Such visits often occur around events such as high school or college reunions, which facilitate the maintenance of these ties (Blieszner & Adams, 1992). Friendships may be primarily commemorative (Rawlins, 1994; see also chap. 2, this volume). For example, commemorative bonds may carry great weight because of shared events earlier in life, such as serving in the military together; "the act of remembering a life period or event maintains contact with people who were important at that time. Such memories perpetuate social bonds and are in turn, sustained by them"

(Elder & Clipp, 1988). Nussbaum (1994) even offered examples of adults in his research who talked about their best friends who had died several years earlier as remaining meaningful and close and to whom they talked everyday.

The third assumption outlined earlier is that long-distance friendships are not as close as proximal relationships. Of course, this is contingent on what "close" means (Johnson, 2001). Berscheid et al. (1989) offered a definition of closeness that includes engaging in joint behaviors. Clearly, if closeness is defined as engaging in joint activities, long-distance friendships are not going to be close by definition (Johnson, Becker, Wigley, Wittenberg, & Haigh, 2003). Johnson et al. (2003) found geographically proximal friends to report joint activities as important for their relational closeness whereas long-distance friends characterized closeness as keeping in touch. However, among college students, proximity was not found to be related to satisfaction, commitment, or feelings of closeness (Johnson, 2001; Johnson et al., 2003; Oswald & Clark, 2003).

This assumption that long-distance friendships are not as close is due to an emphasis on talk. Though talk might be desired, it simply has not been found to be a necessary component of friendships, at least among older adults (Nussbaum, 1994). Though doing things together is arguably a critical component of friendships at some points in life, other criteria for close friendships may be invoked. Closeness in friendships could be considered in numerous ways including support, shared interests, and expressions of the importance of the relationship (Parks & Floyd, 1996).

The focus on emotional closeness and physical proximity brings to light an interesting dialectic of friendships. Friends often report growing apart, yet simultaneously "being there" is "widely cited as a definitive feature of friendship" (Rawlins, 1994, p. 287). Rawlins (1994) considered active friends as those who are expected to be readily available, whereas for other dormant friends, the concept of being there means the "the friendship is there." Yet, dormant friendships may also be reinstantiated to active status in times of need.

Summary

Many assumptions surrounding friendships fundamentally disallow the possibility of close long-distance friendships. Yet, friendships thrive without copresence. This is not to say that long-distance friends would be sufficient. Proximal friendships may not always be best friendships; they are important to life satisfaction. Proximal weak ties meet many companionship needs (Nussbaum, 1994). However, the role of weak ties is often considered secondary. Long-distance friends are sometimes presumed only to be capable of weak ties. However, friendships at a distance do exist, are neither weak nor inherently second class, and meet a myriad of relational needs. Proximity is simply not a criterion for close friendships.

CONCLUSIONS

Friendships and sibships share many commonalities. Each is often characterized as unique, but they are not definitively distinct sets. Childhood or long-term friends can become surrogate or fictive siblings. Siblings can be best friends. Childhood friends share some similarities with some siblings in terms of their duration and shared history. Some childhood friends predate some siblings. Both friends and siblings are primarily conceived as egalitarian relationships; both have somewhat ambiguous roles and definitions. Though siblings are generally considered nonvoluntary relationships, they have been characterized as having many voluntary features, especially after the death of parents. Friendships are characterized as voluntary; however, friends develop kin-like expectations and obligations. Both of these relationships may best be considered on a continuum from voluntary to obligatory.

Close friendships and sibships can be sustained through periods of dormancy with expectations of activation in times of need. Both relationships have a significant influence on our overall well-being, and both take on increasing importance with age. Our proximal networks may serve more functions in our day-to-day lives, but these distant connections, often perpetuated with minimal, if any, interaction, are psychologically and emotionally meaningful.

9

Computer-Mediated LDRs

$\mathbb{B}$y the autumn of 2003, 63% of American adults reported having used the Internet, and 66 million Americans were online in a typical day (Pew Internet & American Life Project, 2003). Going online is not an activity limited to the workplace, though it was originally conceived and implemented as such. In fact, by the autumn of 2003, 87% of U.S. Internet users had home access (Pew Internet & American Life Project, 2003). The primary use of the Internet is e-mail; 90% of online users have sent or received an e-mail (Pew Internet & American Life Project 2004), and in an average day in 2003 more people were online to send or receive e-mail than for any other single purpose (Pew Internet & American Life Project, 2004b). The most common reason for e-mail use from home is for relational purposes (Stafford, Kline, & Dimmick, 1999). Personal and social interaction online also occurs through chat rooms, news-groups, instant messages (IM), and the like.

The coming of age of many new technologies has been met with concern, and the Internet is no different, though some technologies received more re-search attention than others. The telephone for example, has been relatively ig-nored with notable exceptions (e.g., Dimmick, Sikand, & Patterson, 1994; Fischer, 1994). Even when a technological innovation has garnered little atten-tion by social science researchers, debates over the positive or negative effects on family and society often ensue. For example, concerns about the telephone and the automobile have been well documented (see Fischer & Carroll, 1988). The telephone was argued to allow people to connect when visiting FtF was not an option. It was also prophesied to inspire laziness and bring an end to visiting friends in person, thus weakening friendship ties. Similarly, the automobile en-abled visits to friends or relatives in other communities but was also projected to weaken local communities and neighborhoods and to undermine family ties by permitting teenagers to run rampant (Lynd & Lynd, 1929).

Likewise, social and personal ties giving way to alienation and impersonal relationships has been predicted for the Internet age (see Rheingold, 1993). Prophecies of the negative ramifications of Internet use seemed to be fulfilled with reports of isolation or depression among new Internet users (Kraut et al., 1998).

However, these studies have been severely critiqued on methodological and conceptual grounds (Baym, 2002; Walther & Parks, 2002). Some of the same researchers have reversed their initial claims (e.g., Kraut et al., 2002). Moreover, 97% of e-mail users say it has made their life better (Jones, 2001) and the majority say e-mail has increased contact and improved relationships with family members (Pew Internet & American Life Project, 2000a). Walther and Parks (2002) concluded, "Looking across studies to date, it appears that for new Internet users, contact with close ties, as well as social and mental well-being, may suffer slightly while they learn to use the social potential of the Internet. Over time, however, they become adept at using the Internet to maintain contact with friends and family and to obtain social support" (p. 545).

LDRS ONLINE

At the outset of this volume, relationships were considered long distance when communication opportunities are restricted, in the view of the individuals involved, because of geographic parameters, and the individuals within the relationship have expectations of a continued close connection. By invoking the same fuzzy parameters, the contention is made that many relationships that use computer mediated communication (CMC) are long distance.

Three types of LDRs use online modes of interaction. To explain, first consider two types of Internet relationships: those formed offline and those formed online. Relationships may first exist offline and the Internet is then used in conjunction with other traditional media. Certainly, many geographically close relational partners who have unrestricted opportunities for FtF interaction use CMC and other new technologies in addition to FtF interaction. Though copresence is momentarily absent, such relationships would not be considered long distance. But CMC may be one of many modes that individuals in traditional LDRs use to stay in touch. "For those who wish to maintain long-distance contacts with friends and family, however, CMC may be a more satisfying choice than more traditional channels such as letters or the telephone" (Walther & Parks, 2002, p. 545). These traditional LDRs are the first type of LDR in which reliance on CMC is prevalent.

The second and third types are those initiated online. Just as most FtF transactions do not result in a close relationship, neither do most interactions in cyberspace result in a close relationhip. Nonetheless, it is now well established that individuals use numerous types of CMC, such as e-mail, chat rooms, IM, dating sites, and the like for the initiation and development of close personal relationships (e.g., see Parks & Floyd, 1996; Parks & Roberts, 1998).

Two types of relationships initiated online are considered: those that migrate offline and those that remain pure virtual relationships. Either of these patterns (migratory mixed-mode relationships or purely virtual relationships) might be an LDR. When relationships are perceived to be close and are expected to continue, but the individuals have limited access to each other, they are considered as LDRs here, regardless of means of initiation or mode of interaction.

Thus, the three variations of computer-mediated LDRs are traditional long-distance partners who met offline and use CMC as one means of contact, migratory relationships wherein the individuals met online and have engaged in FtF meetings, and pure virtual relationships in which the individuals met online and continue to interact only online. It is recognized that the distinctions among these three patterns are simultaneously meaningful and artificial. The way a relationship forms has an impact on the relationship (Rheingold, 1993). However, mode of origin aside, relational enact- ment is becoming increasingly multimodal (Walther & Parks, 2002). Before directly addressing these three types of online LDRs, a brief description of three major theories relevant to CMC is offered.

THEORETICAL ORIENTATIONS

In an integrative review of theories of CMC, Walther and Parks (2002) noted that given the emphasis placed on physical proximity and physical attraction in relationship initiation and development, both of which are absent in virtual space, traditional theories of relationship formation are inadequate in explaining relationship formation online. They also pointed out that most theories applied to interpersonal interactions online have come from either organizational small-group communication or from theories formed for understanding nondigital media. For overviews of these theories and much more in-depth discussion and consideration of theoretical implications than space allows here, the reader is referred to Baym (2002), Walther and Parks (2002), and Rabby and Walther (2003).

For the most part, neither traditional theories of interpersonal communication nor media are the best way to approach CMC. The framework that has been explicitly developed to explain the development and maintenance of relationships online is the hyperpersonal perspective, thus it is given primary consideration here. Before turning directly to that approach, two other perspectives directly applied to LDRs and CMC are mentioned. These are a uses and gratifications approach (Blumer & Katz, 1974) and a media richness approach (Daft & Lengel, 1984, 1986).

Uses and Gratifications

Uses and gratifications approaches examine the reasons for choice of one media over another; individuals actively seek media best suited to achieve their goals. This approach has been used to explain the rapid adoption of the Internet because of its many advantages (gratifications). E-mail in particular has been found useful for maintaining relationships. Compared with other means, e-mail is seen as superior in its ability to stay in touch with people who live far away in different time zones and is advantageous in speed and cost (Dimmick, Kline, & Stafford, 2000). Though helpful in understanding why individuals apparently like to use e-mail, this approach does not offer much insight into how relationships are maintained.

Media Richness Theory

Two main assumptions of this theory are that people desire to overcome uncertainty, and differing media are inherently more or less rich and are thus differentially suited for different tasks. Rich media allow instantaneous feedback and multiple channels to allow a wide range of cues. In theory, the richer the media, the greater the potential to reduce ambiguity. In this view, FtF communication is the richest communication. This theory suggests that individuals make rational choices matching a particular medium to a specific objective and to the richness that tasks require. Harwood (2000a) applied this perspective to geographically distant grandparent–grandchild relationships, proposing that as grandparent–grandchild relationships are comfortably ambiguous, media low in richness, such as e-mail, are ideally suited means of interfacing (see chap. 8, this volume).

Hyperpersonal Communication

This perspective is an extension of social information processing (SIP) theory (Walther, 1993, 1994). In this view, individuals have the same drive for affiliation online as offline and they adapt cues available to meet relational purposes. Relationships develop more slowly online, but given time, CMC can be as personal as other modes. Walther, Anderson, and Park's (1994) meta-analyses of CMC studies offer general support for the SIP model.

Building on SIP, the hyperpersonal perspective was developed to understand personal relationships and CMC. Individuals take advantage of the lack of cues to project idealized selves online. These cues are selectively adhered to and influence the messages returned, which are also manipulated to present positive pictures of self. Thus, interactions can quickly become positively "hyperpersonal." This perspective is invoked in discussion of idealization in computer-mediated relationships.

TYPES OF COMPUTER-MEDIATED LDRS

Pure Virtual Relationships

Most research on CMC has examined pure virtual relationships (Rabby & Walther, 2003). Initially, the idea that close relationships could develop online was met with skepticism, but several reports provide evidence that close relationships could and do form in virtual reality. For example, 90% of individuals participating in online multiuser discussions reported forming a deep personal relationship with someone they met online (Parks & Floyd, 1996). Approximately 25% of Internet users report having made friends with someone they met online, and this figure has remained remarkably constant since 1995 (Pew Internet & American Life Project, 2000a). Most scholars now accept that close bonds can form through CMC (McKenna & Bargh, 2000); thus, the features of CMC and communicative practices that allow such development are beginning to be examined (e.g., McKenna, Green, & Gleason, 2002; Ramirez, Walther, Burgoon, & Sunnafrank, 2002; Tidwell & Walther, 2002).

Before a relationship can be formed people must meet; the internet expands the sheer number of people one can encounter (Lea & Spears, 1995). Individuals may bump into each other in variety of forums from asynchronous postings in newsgroups or bulletin boards to the synchronous communication in multiuser discussion groups (Rabby & Walther, 2003). When one participates in a group dedicated to a specific topic there is the assumption of some commonalities. Thus, in some ways relationships begin the same way FtF relationships do; people meet because they have something in common (Rabby & Walther, 2003).

Ways to learn about others online is limited. As a result, people have become resourceful in adapting to the medium to gather information about others (Walther & Parks, 2002). In CMC individuals ask more questions, and more personal questions, and offer more and deeper self-disclosure on more intimate topics than in FtF meetings (Tidwell & Walther, 2002). Interpretations are derived from a combination of the content of the message, the time it is sent, and the speed of reply (Walther & Parks, 2002). For instance, during the day, prompt replies to task-oriented message are interpreted as more affectionate than task messages sent at night. This pattern is reversed for social messages (Tidwell & Walther, 2002).

Time and speed of response are not the only noncontent cues. In efforts to indicate emotional states and provide partners with cues for interpretation of a message, emoticons are sometimes used (Walther & Tidwell, 1995). Emoticons are typed text characters representing facial expressions turned sideways. Basic examples include : -) as a smile indicating happiness or sarcasm and : -(as a frown of unhappiness. Intentions aside, limited research on emoticons indicate that positive ones have little impact on the recipient of the message, whereas negative ones carry some weight (Walther & D'Addario, 2001).

Other conventions are also used in efforts to guide interpretations such as acronyms, like lol (laughing out loud) and typing in all capital letters to indicate SHOUTING. typing in all lower case letters may be interpreted as laziness, but among close friends, this may be taken positively (Rabby & Walther, 2003). Just how such features actually function in terms of message interpretation is unknown.

Another facet of CMC is its relative anonymity. Users have the ability to manage identity and carefully construct messages should they choose to do so. When interchanges are asynchronous, the channel affords the ability to edit and revise messages, thus allowing even greater control over self-presentation.

Teenagers often develop different personalities to mold their identities for mischievous purposes (Pew Internet & American Life Project, 2001b); adults tend to manipulate the truth about their age, appearance, or employment (Walther & Parks, 2002). Though socially deviant misrepresentations for ill-fraught purposes occur in virtual reality, much misrepresentation takes place to present an idealized representation of self.

Drawing from Goffman (1959), Cornwell and Lundgren (2001) argued that individuals generally tend to present themselves in favorable idealized ways; the Internet simply allow peoples to do so more readily. Physical appearance, so greatly influential in FtF relational initiation, is usually unavailable to those who encounter each other online. However, new technologies such as webcams provide a means of seeing each other, and although people like to see whom they are interacting with, they do not like to be seen. Moreover, the use of such technologies is still limited in the United States. When people meet online they are offered the luxury of discovering similarities of values and interests, and conversational style, without the accompanying concern of physical appearance (McKenna & Bargh, 2000).

In general, relationship development feeds on cycles of interactions, and online relationships are no exception. As selective messages of the other's positive self-presentation are received, selective messages are sent in return. Relationships emerge as individuals overattribute commonalities and positive impressions, leading to idealized visions of partners (Walther, Slovacek, & Tidwell, 2001). The caption under a cartoon in the New Yorker of two dogs sitting in front of a computer read, "On the internet no one knows you're a dog" (Steiner, 1993). This phrase captures this ability to alter self-presentation.

Migrating Offline

One vision of the world online is that of a dangerous collection of deviants wait-ing to prey on unsuspecting victims. Strong feelings of distrust permeate most Internet users (Pew Internet & American Life Project, 2001b). Yet, only 4% of Internet users report ever having felt threatened online, and overall, individuals behave in trusting ways online (Pew Internet & American Life Project, 2000b). Of course, socially deviant interactions do occur and can cross over into physical reality. For example, cyberstalking has been reported to lead to some instances of stalking in real life. Though this type of movement from online to offline is rare, it does not lessen the very real and often traumatic experiences of victims (see Finn & Banach, 2000; Spitzberg & Hoobler, 2002).

At the other extreme are romanticized visions of love online. In the first 6 months of 2003, $214.3 million was reported to be spent on online personal ads and dating sites (Egan, 2003). This outlay of money is by a comparatively small group of people. Only 8% of individuals who go online have ever visited a dating Web site, and in a typical day only 1% of online individuals had the express pur-pose of meeting someone new (Pew Internet & American Life Project, 2004).

The use of the Internet for online dating, though romanticized in the ab-stract, carries a social stigma. It is seen as the last resort for the desperate (Lea & Spears, 1995). As the Internet is used for more and more aspects of life, it re-mains to be seen if meeting romantic partners online retains this stigma. Al-though about 50% of those using an online dating service moved offline to a FtF meeting (Cornwell & Lundgren, 2001), relatively few individuals in romantic rela-tionships formed online first met through dating services, or even with the in-tent of meeting a romantic partner. Rather, meetings occur through online discussions (Baker, 2002).

In fact, neither dangerous nor romantic migrations are typical. Innocuous friendships comprise the majority of offline introductions (e.g., see Knox et al., 2002; Parks & Floyd, 1996). When relationships transfer to other modes, they seldom go directly to FtF encounters. Rather, the vast majority of individuals go through other media first. For example, friendships moved from discussion groups, to individual e-mail, telephone, cards and letters, and even photo-graphs, before a FtF encounter (Parks & Roberts, 1996).

The exchange of photos poses an interesting dilemma and has sometimes been found to dampen relationships (Walther et al., 2001). Others have re-ported that exchanging photos was of little importance as they had already grown to care for each other; they came to know each other "from the inside out" (Baker, 2002).

The FtF meeting is a more critical turning point in relationships that even the exchange of photographs. Expectations may be high and inaccuracies in self-presentation addressed. When individuals face each other in the flesh, discontinuities between the virtual identity and the bodily identity must be reconciled (Walther & Parks, 2002). Why some friendships or romances survive this transformation and others do not is not well understood. It is likely that expectations, extent of discrepancy between virtual and actual characteristics, and the strength of the bond before the FtF engagement play at least some role in successfully crossing into "real life."

CMC in Traditional LDRs

A high-profile example of CMC for relational connectivity comes from the hours immediately after the attack on New York's Twin Towers on September 11, 2001. In the 48 hours following the event, 4 to 5 million people used the Internet to connect with friends and loved ones (Pew Internet & American Life Project, 2001a). Most online contact is not this dramatic. Individuals routinely go online simply to stay in touch with people with whom they already have an offline relationship (Huges & Hans, 2001).

It has been proposed that traditional LDRs and online relationships are radically different social forms (Adams, 1998). Yet, how CMC is used within relationships previously formed through FtF interaction has attracted minimal attention. This is surprising, as already mentioned, most e-mail users report more interaction with family after beginning online interaction with those family members. A significant amount of Internet traffic is dedicated to contact among family members and friends.

The use of IM for relational maintenance among long-distance friends and family is beginning to receive attention. It has been proposed that the features of IM, in conjunction with other modes of interaction, render it a viable means of relational maintenance, and those who use it rely on it for maintaining multiple relationships such as a romantic partner, numerous friends, and some family relationships (Ramirez & Broneck, in press).

Studies of CMC use among traditional LDRs, when available, were mentioned in prior chapters. With notable exceptions (e.g., Harwood's (2000a) consideration of media richness theory in grandparent–grandchild interaction) research has been atheoretical and predominantly focused only on frequency of contact with the assumption that frequency of contact is good and the use of CMC simply provides a viable additional means of contact. CMC use is often pragmatic. Access and gratifications approach stresses the advantages of e-mail among friends, family, and loved ones at a distance. It is faster than a letter and cheaper than long-distance phone calls, differing time zones are unimportant, and individuals can read and respond with this asynchronous mode at their own convenience (Dimmick et al., 2000).

The role of CMC among those who already know each other may be contingent on the relationship and additional modes of interaction. Those who are already well acquainted and see each other often may use CMC differently from those for whom CMC is the predominant mode of interaction. CMC would not be expected to alter drastically the relationships among those who already have close relationships with frequent FtF interaction. In these instances, computer-mediated messages might resemble the banal, mundane small talk that Duck (1994a) has characterized as the essence of everyday relational life (Rabby & Walther, 2003). However, if these relationships become predominantly mediated, as in the case of many traditional LDRs, hyperpersonal interaction may become more likely (Walther & Parks, 2002). When CMC is the primary means of contact, and FtF or other forms of interaction are sparse, messages tend to promote positive illusions (Gunn & Gunn, 2000; Rabby & Walther, 2003).

CMC may encourage both idealization and maintenance of romantic relationships. Romantic partners use e-mail to stay in touch, and simply sending a CMC message lets the other know the relationship exists and the other is being thought about (Rabby & Walther, 2003). E-mail messages among romantic partners are seldom, if ever, negative (Rabby, 1997). Arguments, are not frequent online and are usually reserved for FtF interactions or for telephone conversations (Rabby & Walther, 2003). E-mail messages place an emphasis on the positive and contribute to idealized images and expectations, in a manner similar to letters. "When one communicates largely through e-mail he or she loses the sense of that partner's ... undesirable habits" (Rabby & Walther, 2003, p. 154).

CONCLUSIONS

In 1995, Lea and Spears bemoaned the dearth of studies on CMC and personal relationships. Since that time, "the simple picture of CMC and its effects painted by early experimental research has given way to a far more varied and complex portrait, or set of portraits, as the use of CMC has grown and people have found new ways to make use of it" (Baym, 2002, p. 71).

Rabby and Walther (2003) insightfully noted that whether CMC is harmful or helpful is the most asked question, and the answer is that it is both. More important, this is not the best question to be pursued. "Rather than to look for the drastic changes media are unlikely to produce, we urge the curious to look for the subtleties, the surprises, the delights, and fluctuations promise to teach us little about media but a lot about how humans pursue relationships, no matter how many miles of geography or network connections lie between them" (p. 159).

Communication research has tended to dichotomize relationships as either FtF or virtual and comparisons between the two are made. However, this is artificial, as those who meet online may migrate offline and "it is increasingly common for people to use the Internet as one among many channels for communication with work partners, social partners, and family members" (Walther & Parks, 2002, p. 556). Media scholars and relational scholars from many domains can inform each other. Insular inspection only serves to constrain our understanding of the increasing complexities of the ways relationships and media intersect.

10

Propositions, Implications, Limitations, and Lacunae

Scholars of early research on geographic mobility reached the conclusion that individuals maintain relationships with friends and families left physically behind. However, attention turned to the establishment of new relationships in new locales of the geographically mobile family rather than the contin- uance of their previous ties (Adams, 1998). Thus, research and theory on nonproximal relationships and cross-residential families lag behind research on geographi- cally close relationships and coresidential families. Also, research is scattered across fields of study. This book has been an effort to bring together this limited and disjointed literature base.

LDRs and cross-residential relationships have been presented as existing in opposition to one or more general beliefs about the nature of communication or relationships. These assumptions are articulated in chapter 2: (a) Frequent FtF communication is necessary for close relationships, (b) geographic proxim- ity is necessary for close relationships, (c) families are supposed to share resi- dences, and (d) shared meanings are necessary for close relationships.

However, examination of the literature surrounding long-distance and cross-residential kin and friendship ties leads to different conclusions. Neither frequent contact, FtF interaction, nor geographic proximity is necessary to maintain close relationships. Family members need not live under one roof. Al- though relational partners certainly have meanings for their relationships, and these meanings were formed (and can continue to be reformed) through inter- action, talk is not always necessary, meanings do not always have to be shared, and understanding does not always need to be reached for successful close re- lational continuation. Rather, cognitive distortions, via positive illusions, imagined interactions, and faulty memories often sustain LDRs. These intertwined ideas are integrated to forward propositional conclusions.

PROPOSITIONAL CONCLUSIONS

The preceding literature leads to several conclusions about the role of communication and social cognition in close relationships. Specifically:

- A lack of interaction can promote positive relational realities.
- Interaction can promote negative relational realities.
- Shared meaning and understanding are achieved through interaction and are simultaneously necessary for relationships, unimportant to relationships, and destructive to relationships.

These inextricably linked propositions are explicated in the next few pages.

A prime reason for everyday talk is "because it continues to embody partner's understanding or shared meaning" (Duck, 1994b, p. 54). Talk forms understanding, shared meanings, and the relationship itself. "The total of the relational partners' view of their relationship contributes to the maintenance of their relationship" (Masuda & Duck, 2002, p. 23). However, LDRs do not have everyday talk, even if they do have frequent mediated contact.

In geographically close relationships, individual relational representations can be derived based on considerably more information than in LDRs. Relational meanings and memories of relationships (including, or perhaps especially, distorted memories), though formed on the basis of interaction, can sustain relationships during separations.

A distinction has been drawn between cognitive-based idealizations and behavior-based idealizations (Miller, Caughlin, & Huston, 2003). Some illusions are formed through cognitive exaggerations of partners' positive points and minimization of negative points. However, some illusions develop because of a limited range of behavior on which to draw conclusions (behavioral idealizations) rather than because the partner exaggerates positive features or overlooks negative features (cognitive idealization). "Idealization may partly reflect the fact that spouses are not privy to the entire behavior repertoire of their partners. Obviously, this is quite a different notion of idealization from that proffered in earlier research" (Miller et al., 2003, p. 992).

The claim that behavioral idealization has gone previously unrecognized is highly debatable. Schulman (1974), for example, proposed that romantic couples maintain positive, unrealistic images of each other by circumventing the discussion of areas of potential conflict, that is, limiting exposure of selected features. The labels *cognitive* and *behavioral* idealization, though, are welcome as they allow for greater ease in discussion.

Clearly, idealizations of both kinds operate in LDRs. Cognitive idealization occurs as partners' faults recede into the background and positive illusions come to the forefront. LDRs afford optimal conditions for the development and continuance of behavioral distortions, as has been argued throughout this volume. Restriction occurs both in terms of the sheer amount of interaction time and the nature of the conversation and behavior presented.

Long-distance partners tend put their best face forward when together in dating and marital relationships. They also tend to avoid areas of disagreement when separated; conversations are filled with relational assurances. Similarly, adult siblings avoid conflictual topics to sustain affection. Inmates often have only pictures of their children from which to envision them and daydream of rejoining their children. Military personnel may receive only positive, vague letters or e-mails. Individuals present idealized images of self through CMC. Because this is the type of data available to individuals in LDRs, it is little wonder that idealization results.

Limited communication appears to promote positive illusions, and positive illusions have been found to promote relational stability (Murray & Holmes, 1996). As discussed in chapter 4, this idealization may account for the relative stability of long-distance dating relationships. Benevolent misunderstandings also contribute to relational maintenance. Individuals desire to misunderstand each other to lessen the threat of facing disagreement or discussing an uncomfortable topic (Simpson et al., 1995). Idealistic distortion sustains and enhances romantic relationships (Rusbult et al., 2001). It also fosters affection among long-distance relatives.

Daily presence allows for greater interaction; concurrently, then, the potential to uncover areas of disagreement is also greater. Idealized images may be increasingly difficult to sustain in day-to-day interaction (Bochner, 1984). In other words, the potential for interaction to lead to accuracy or understanding of another, and hence relational dissatisfaction, must be taken into account (Bochner, 1982).

Such views are well accepted when considering dating relationships in the abstract. Through dating people attempt to get to know each other; they often discover areas of incompatibility that lead to relational dissatisfaction and termination. Nevertheless, sustaining the relationship is thought of as success. Morever, why the idea that increased interaction and subsequent understanding in kinships, friendships, or committed romantic unions, or even between parents and children, would automatically lead to better relationships is a mystery. Interaction risks uncovering unpleasant relational truths.

Optimistic distortion only becomes problematic when reality is thrust on relational participants. Unrealistic images of the partner and the time they will have together swell with absence leading to disillusionment and disappointment (Gerstel & Gross, 1984). Among civilian couples, the reunion is greatly anticipated, and then, after an initial honeymoon high, sometimes coupled with feelings of awkwardness and getting reacquainted, a time of conflict and alignment of roles ensues (Gross, 1980). Studies of military personnel report similar findings (Wood et al., 1995), as do those of long-distance dating couples (Sahlstein, 2004). The danger in idealization is that, if reunited, the risk of expectations exceeding enactment is incurred and inaccurate images may be shattered.

Shared understandings are simply of no consequence in some relationships. Jointly held relational meanings are of absolutely no importance in relationships that will be continued only in thought, as many commemorative relationships are. Also, as long as latent relationships remain passive, differing relational views are unproblematic and even facilitative. However, if one has an expectation that a friend will be there in a time of need and the friend does not define the relationship the same way, problems occur if, and only if, the friend is actually called on.

In other words, taken-for-granted relational constructions are problematic when misalignment of meanings become salient. Schutz (1964) described "the homecomer ... (who) expects to return to an environment of which ... he thinks (he) still has intimate knowledge which he has just to take for granted in order to find his bearings" (p. 106). When partners entertain grossly differing views of their relationship, perhaps even different views as to whether their relationship has been redefined or even exists, a quandary results. This is illustrated by the example in chapter 6 when a father comes home from prison to find his child does not know him and perceives someone else as daddy.

PRACTICAL IMPLICATIONS

As noted in chapter 2, not only do LDRs provide the opportunity to test and develop theory, they also offer scholars an opportunity to develop applied research to aid in the formulation of policies and intervention in multiple domains. Some implications for practice are offered next.

College Dating Relationships

Though long-term studies are lacking, preliminary data suggest that many college long-distance dating relationships run into difficulty when they become geographically close (Stafford et al., 2004). Considering the probable level of idealization, a difficult transition to daily interaction should be of little surprise. But apparently it is of great surprise to some. The following excerpts from narratives of long-distance college dating partners who moved to the same location indicate some of the difficulties: "After spending more face-to-face time we began fighting more often. I stopped looking forward to our time together. He was someone I didn't really know"; "She had changed in ways I could not deal with "; "Before we didn't see each other as often, so being annoyed with each other was not frequent" (Stafford et al., 2004, p. 23).

Thus, although young adults generally desire to know how to make their romantic relationships last, facilitating the acquisition of knowledge to allow more realistic relational decisions may be more important. Recommendations are that partners should attempt to know each other well through increased small talk and not avoid potential areas of disagreement that must be reconciled at some point. "Practitioner's goals are not always therefore to prevent relationship dissolution, but also to establish whether dissolution may in fact be a better option" (Masuda & Duck, 2002, p. 32).

Adult Romantic Relationships

Though more contact is often desired between long-distance partners, it has not been found to be particularly helpful unless it is simply vaguely positive, such as an affirmation of the relationship. When a family member is made aware of difficulties those at home are facing and is unable to help, morale is lowered or a sense of helplessness ensues. For military personnel, detailed contact, especially about problems, tends to result in feelings of helplessness and difficulty enacting military duties. Some DCDR couples report that talking on the telephone makes their loneliness worse. Thus, symbolic representations may be more satisfactory.

Ironically, many of the same mechanisms that allow for successful absences, such as idealized visions, acting autonomously, and relying heavily on local support networks, may impede successful unification as interdependence with the partner decreases substantially. Thus, the ability to be highly adaptable to cycles of departure, absence, and return is critical.

Such cycles may be eased through joint planning for the departure as well as the return. Negotiation in advance of roles and expectations for the absence may ease transitions. Engagement in behaviors before departure that project relational continuance during the departure, features that reinforce the continuance during separation (such as photographs), and activities or traditions that recognize the reconstitution of a physically present relationship may be helpful (see chap. 11, this volume, on continuity units).

Civilians separated for occupational or educational reasons have the most voluntary control over their situations. Separations before having children or after they are grown are advised, as opposed to separating when children are young. Being physically close enough so that the commute is not demanding as well as attempting to locate flexible positions also seems helpful.

For military families and those with an incarcerated member, some form of positive or nurturing contact or even mere one-way information from home such as an uplifting letter, care packages, or news relayed through others simply to say that their family is doing well is associated with positive outlooks and alleviates loneliness (Segrin & Flora, 2001; Ursano & Norwood, 1996). Families of inmates and military personnel seem to adjust better when information about their absent family member is available. Thus, military and institutional efforts to keep families apprised of the status of their absent member decreases some stress. Support systems among individuals in similar situations also appear to be helpful.

PARENTS AND YOUNG CHILDREN

Cross-Residential Parents and Children

Despite the pervasive opinion that contact between nonresidential children and their parents is always good, this appears to be far from the case. When parents cooperate and keep conflict at a minimum or at least hidden from the children, and children truly share their time in the homes of both parents, the parents and the children benefit (Buchanan, 2000; Buchanan et al., 1996; Kelly, 2000). Unequivocally, fathers who remain positively involved in children's lives and entertain a collegial relationship with the other parent contribute to the adjustment and happiness of the children (DeFrain & Olson, 1999). Though research on nonresidential mothers is limited, it seems the same logic would apply.

This suggests parent–child relationships may best be facilitated by improving the coparental relationship. Simply mandating joint custody, hence joint decision making, does not accomplish this goal; when the parents remain hostile this arrangement can actually be detrimental to the child (Emery, 1994). In addition, helping nonresidential parents view their role as a parent as distinct from a role that was previously parent and partner may facilitate positive parent–child involvement.

Parental Absence

Incarceration, selected occupations, and military duty also separate parents and children. Children of prisoners are 6 times more likely to become criminals than children in the general population (Reed & Reed, 1997). Given that violent criminals are predominately males who grew up without fathers (Brenner, 2001), speculation has been offered that because paternal imprisonment separates children from fathers, incarceration may be feeding a cycle of criminal behavior into the next generation as opposed to curbing it (Davidson, 1990).

Arditti et al. (2003) argued that current penal policies create more harm than good and alternative policies and approaches need to be adopted; given the negative family and societal ramifications of the current penal system, imprisonment should be considered a last resort. Rather than imprisonment, an emphasis should be on harm reduction and intervention (Lenton, 2003). Restorative justice models ensure that incarceration does no more harm than the crime and concentration is shifted to intervention (Arditti et al., 2003).

Research on the relationship between traveling civilian parents and their children is missing. As noted earlier, children have been of interest in terms of whether their presence or age creates difficulties for the couple. When the children are the focal point, the central concern has been on potential negative effects of parental absence rather than on enhancing the parent–child bond.

Some practices may help maintain affectionate ties, such as a symbolic parental presence, rituals, and parental acknowledgment of special occasions. Allowing age-appropriate control over as many circumstances as possible surrounding the separation, adhering to appropriate boundaries and family roles at home, and receiving reasonable support by local networks may also help.

Relationships Among Adult Kinships and Friends

Limited research leads to limited practical advice concerning adult kin relationships. Perhaps a reason for the lack of research on maintaining kin relationships is, as Bedford and Bleiszner (2000) claimed, that kin relationships are givens. The obligatory nature of adult kinship allows for the maintenance of LDRs more readily than among voluntary ties (Wellman & Wortley, 1989). Although, some have proposed that the obligatory nature of kinships is lessening (Johnson, 2000), it remains to be seen to what extent and under what circumstances family roles and relations are indeed shifting from duty to choice, or if indeed they are shifting at all. For now, scholars generally concur that family membership entails certain expectations.

As discussed in chapter 8, adult kinships and friendships are often maintained across significant durations. Cards or letters, telephone, and e-mail can reinforce relationships, as can occasional reunions. Other times, relationships are sustained through memories. It may be the lack of interaction that facilitates the continuance of these relationships as meaningful. If individuals perceive a relationship is latent but can be called on, this goes a long way in sustaining perceptions of closeness and positive affect.

Middle-aged adults are cautioned to avoid contributing to feelings of dependency by the older parents, who desire to retain an independent life style.

Mere acceptance of a young adult child as a young *adult* whether at home or away seems to promote ties. Siblings may consider affirming their relationships given the comfort afforded by the simple knowledge that one has a sibling. Both long-distance friendships and sibships may be promoted by reciprocal acknowledgment that each would indeed be there in times of need.

Adult grandchildren are advised to be the initiator of contact, as that which occurs without parental prompting is seen as more meaningful. Grandparents who desire close relationships with grandchildren must accept a role that often means by societal standards that they are "old" in a negative sense. Grandparents should attempt to minimize areas of tension with their grandchildren's parents as they are the gatekeepers to the grandchildren when young. As e-mail is a major means of correspondence among young adults, and it may be especially suited for grandparent–grandchild relationships, grandparents would be well advised to adopt this medium.

Obviously, much more applied research is needed in all domains of LDRs. Despite the absence of research-based advice, bookstores and Web sites offering help with LDRs abound. A quick Google search on the term "long-distance relationship advice" yielded approximately 200,000 sites. The same parameters on Amazon resulted in 70,000 listings. These numbers dwarf the academic research publications on this topic.

LIMITATIONS AND LACUNAE

The study of LDRs is plagued with problems. The most striking feature is its scarcity. The extant research is typified by little theoretical guidance, a lack of focus on mechanisms of relational maintenance, a limited array of relational forms, a deficit of cultural considerations, and a myriad of unquestioned and untested assumptions.

Collaboration across disciplines is needed. Theoretical perspectives typically applied to relational communication do not adequately address LDRs. Most LDRs are enacted, at least in part, through some type of mediated communication, whether letters, telephone, or CMC. Yet, concomitant with relational scholars' neglect of media, scholars of mediated interaction predominantly ignore the manner in which media are invoked to maintain relationships. Personal relationship scholars, as a group, seem to forget that relationships do continue after a FtF encounter has ended; media scholars, as a group, seem to forget that actual people are on either end of the computer terminal.

When the fields of media and personal relationships have intersected, preoccupation has been with the initiation of online relationships and their subsequent development, and how such relationships might be similar or different to those formed through FtF interactions (Walther & Parks, 2002). This tells us little about how individuals in relationships formed offline use mediated interaction to sustain their relationships.

The previous pages have concentrated on a relatively narrow domain of relationships. In the Introduction it was noted that LDRs contradict U.S. cultural expectations for both communication in close relationships and for structural living arrangements. Worldwide, these expectations are far from universally held and even further from universally enacted. For example, South Africa has numerous families living apart because of the migrant labor system as well the number of married live-in domestics who must live apart from their families (Le Roux, 1995; Viljoen, 1994). In Japan, some corporate employees are expected to relocate without their families for periods of 3 to 5 years; as of 1992, 3.5 million Japanese resided temporarily in North America. Though some are accompanied by families, a significant number are not (Shwalb, Imaizumi, & Nakazawa, 1987). Even when families relocate to another country as a group, friends and other relatives are left behind (Hiew, 1992).

The extent to which LDRs violate cultural expectancies varies drastically. For example, estimates indicate that 41% of all couples in central Thailand live apart after marriage because of the high proportion of seasonal or temporary jobs (Rindfuss, Chamratrithirong, & Morgan, 1988). These individuals, usually males, live away from their home region, spouses, children, and friends for years, returning weekly, monthly, yearly, or on a seasonal basis (Golum Quddus, 1992). Assistance to the wife and family at home is provided by community members and extended family. Given that the extended family is identified as the fundamental unit in Thailand (Seefeldt & Keawkungwal, 1986), coupled with the impracticality of moving the entire family (Golum Quddus, 1992), the migratory husband is not in conflict with societal expectations.

Care also must be taken in not to overgeneralize about cultural expectations or long-distance families in the United States. For example, patterns of dual residence and reliance on extended family and fictive kin has been noted among Hispanic migratory farm workers in the United States. The spouse and children at home also rely on extended family in the husband's absence. Some migratory workers desire to return eventually to their families because providing for the families needs in the United States is not a viable option. Others plan to bring wives and children and other family members to the United States at a future point (Suarez, 1998).

Immigration to the United States centers on political and socioeconomic debates. When research has considered the migratory individual or family, concerns are with adaptation or assimilation. Little attention has been paid to the maintenance of relationships with individuals who have not come to the United States (Hernandez & McGoldrick, 1999).

We have barely begun to tap the multitude of differences or similarities among long-distance forms, and some LDRs remain completely unstudied. The literature on long-distance grandparents and grandchildren focuses on young adults. How relationships are developed among nonproximal grandparents and young grandchildren is unaddressed. Research on committed adult unions, other than heterosexual marriage, is noticeably absent, as is consideration of LDRs between young adults who do not attend college and their parents or grandparents. Children may also be separated from their parents because of placement in foster homes, juvenile facilities, or boarding or preparatory schools. In short, the list of relational configurations not considered is much longer than those considered, though isolated studies have been conducted in some of the aforementioned areas. Yet, studies are certainly not prevalent and suffer from the same problems already enumerated in terms of limited theory and conceptual confusion.

Also, it must be recognized that even similar relationship types have important distinctions. For example, DCDR marriages wherein partners choose to live apart to optimize individual self-fulfillment of both spouses are met with skepticism, especially if young children are involved. It is more acceptable for men to be away from their partners and children for extended periods. Military marriages cannot be conceived as uniform either. Differences exist between active duty personnel and reservists; between those deployed in combat versus noncombat units; and among dual-career, single-career, or single-parent military families. Children who live away from a parent face different issues pending the nature of the separation; there is little similarity among children of DCDR executives and those of incarcerated individuals in terms of social stigma, socioeconomic status, or opportunities for interaction with their parents. Divorced nonresidential parents may disappear from their children's lives, perpetuate hostilities, or cooperatively coparent children. The stress or depression encountered by a college student or member of a DCDR marriage simply cannot be compared to that encountered by the spouse of a deployed soldier in combat. Each LDR has different barriers to overcome in attempts to sustain desired relational features and different degrees or types of stress.

Finally, views of family relationships beyond assumptions of the joint residence of two married heterosexual adults with 1.7 young biological children, an SUV, and a dog, living close (but not too close) to two sets of biological married, heterosexual grandparents must be recognized as these represent only a small number of kin relationships. Consider the interwoven networks of stepparent(s) and a child's first parents. "For the adults, challenges include maintaining ties with children from previous relationships, continuing to coparent with a former spouse or partner, and developing and maintaining relationships with new partners and perhaps stepchildren. Stepchildren are faced with maintaining ties with nonresidential parents, and perhaps nonresidential siblings, while developing and maintaining relationships with one or more stepparents and stepsiblings" (Ganong, Coleman, & Weaver, 2002, p. 125). Residentially and genetically bound nucleocentric views of families obfuscate understanding of how real family relationships are structured and conducted.

CONCLUSIONS

As has been a theme throughout, actual communication is seldom studied in LDRs. When communication is the focus of study, it is often merely the frequency of contact, particularly FtF contact. Of course, it is, and always has been, absurd to equate frequency of communication with closeness of relationships, yet as Parks (1995) has made clear, this frequent FtF communication is seen as a must for close relationships. Parks acknowledged that such beliefs are beginning to dissipate from the thinking of many relational researchers. A notable base of scholars of personal relationships have moved away from the blanketed prescriptions for increased communication as a relational panacea (e.g., see Baxter & Montgomery, 1996).

Yet, such perceptions remain firmly implanted in most undergraduate texts and popular culture. Based on the priority, across multiple academic disciplines, granted sheer quantity of contact, it appears to be valued above all else for relational closeness. Frequency of contact has even been considered an index of, if not synonymous with, close relational bonds. In spite of this, findings indicate that neither frequency nor FtF communication are defining hallmarks of relational maintenance or success (however success might be conceived).

11

Toward an Expanded Vision of Relational Maintenance

$\mathbb{F}$ollowing Stafford and Canary's (1991) initial foray into the application of equity theory to relational maintenance, each has continued separately, together, and with colleagues to extend, elaborate, and explicate this work (for reviews of the development of this program see Canary & Stafford, 1994a, 2001; Canary & Zelley, 2000; Stafford, 2003). Individuals in LDRs have been included in some of their research or research invoking this paradigm, yet specific consideration of LDRs remains largely unaddressed (however, see Dainton & Aylor, 2001, 2002; Johnson, 2001, on college student LDRs). Moreover, active relationships (as opposed to latent or commemorative relationships) have been presumed. Voluntary relationships have been privileged over involuntary ones (however, see Dainton, 2003). Extensions to this program of work are offered to allow application to LDRs (including cross-residential relationships), nonvoluntary relationships, and latent and commemorative relationships. The basic propositions as outlined by Canary and Stafford (1994b, pp. 7–10) are:

1. All relationships require maintenance behaviors or else they deteriorate.
2. People are more motivated to maintain equitable relationships than inequitable ones.
3. Maintenance activities vary according to the development and type of the relationship.
4. Maintenance behaviors may be used in isolation or in combination to variously affect the nature of the relationship.
5. Maintenance is both interactive and noninteractive.

6. People use both strategic (intentional) and routine (unintentional) means to maintain their relationships.[7]

Modifications or elaborations of relevant propositions are offered in turn.

The first proposition is in need of revision and clarification to adopt explicitly Duck's (1988) two-pronged assumption concerning relational maintenance. This assumption states that relationships must be maintained or they will end, and yet, paradoxically, relationships will continue unless something happens to cause their demise. Although Canary and Stafford (1994b) acknowledged the latter forces by stating, "Without maintenance behaviors, the forces pulling dyads apart are generally more powerful than barriers keeping dyads together" (p. 7), they privileged the former.

Nonetheless, it is not proposed that these forces are equal; differing relational forms and circumstances likely call for more reliance on one force or the other. For example, it is proposed that relationships characterized as relatively obligatory as opposed to voluntary, or latent or commemorative as opposed to active are generally least in need of active relational maintenance mechanisms. The relational forms alluded to are not mutually exclusive. For example, some relationships are long distance, obligatory, and latent. The extent to which LDRs require active or interactive maintenance depends much on other relational parameters. Recall the argument in chapter 2 that some relationships are maintained, or at least their existence is, by their societally recognized structures. Such relationships may have obligatory barriers holding them together (Hess, 2003). These relationships may classify as those labeled by Dainton (2003) as involuntary and unintentionally maintained.

The second and third propositions are considered conjointly. Though equity has been forwarded as a universal, the extent to which it is proposed to operate in nonvoluntary family forms has been questioned (Vogl-Bauer, 2003). Clearly, perceptions of equity operate in nonvoluntary relationships, as was illustrated by the example of siblings who report inequity in caring for elderly parents. Yet it is possible that nonvoluntary relationships tolerate greater inequity than voluntary relationships. Leaving the relationship is not an option. The relationship simply continues. However, whether such relationships are characterized by their preferred features is a different question. Siblings, parents and children, and other kin continue connections indefinitely, and feelings of hostility or distress may coexist with affection and security.

In addition, various relationships have differing standards for equity. Unlike some social exchange approaches that maximize profits, perceptions of fair-

---

[7]Stafford (2003) questioned the use of the terms *strategic* and *routine*. Following suit, Dainton (2003) has proposed the labels of *intentional and unintentional*.

ness are at the center of equity theory (Perlman, 2001). Modifying one's base of comparison is a way to restore equity (Adams, 1965; Walster et al., 1973). For example, adolescents have been found to be more satisfied with their family when they are overbenefited as compared with their parents (Vogl-Bauer, Kalbfleisch, & Beatty, 1999). This makes perfect sense from a family solidarity perspective as well as an equity perspective: Parents and children invoke differing criteria, changing bases for comparison, to determine what is fair. Thus, the first three propositions in conjunction yield the following:

In selected relational contexts, forces sustaining desired relational definitions are as strong, if not more so, than forces tearing away at these definitions.

The fourth and fifth propositions assert that multiple maintenance mechanisms may work together and these mechanisms may be interactive or noninteractive. Though not discussed here, Canary and Stafford (1993) have included personality dispositions as one noninteractive force in relational maintenance. They have also proposed that certain behaviors, such as doing one's fair share of instrumental tasks, may be completed individually. The domain of noninteractive means of maintenance is expanded here to include cognitions and societal structures. Cognitions may be invoked in combination with other maintenance behaviors.

Consideration of cognitive processes is consistent with equity theory. Cognitive distortions have been proposed as one way to rectify inequity (Adams, 1965; Walster et al., 1973). Though argued to be difficult to sustain (Sprecher, 1986), it is proposed here that idealization may enable such distortions.

Moreover, distortions are not limited to visions of equity. Perceptual distortion may be the primary means of maintenance among latent or commemorative relationships. Distortion is more likely in LDRs, even when active, than geographically close relationships because of the restricted communication as discussed in chapter 9. In this way, a lack of interaction, or high levels of mediated interaction in the absence of FtF interaction, coupled with positively distorted imagines serve maintenance functions. Pleasant, affectionate memories or daydreaming have been reported as ways to continue desired relational definitions. Societal structures as forces holding together relationships was discussed earlier.

Long-distance partners may simply have fewer opportunities to enact certain behaviors; unfortunately, Stafford and Canary's (1991) focus on frequency of maintenance behaviors has unintentionally resulted in frequency being equated with importance. The idea that some behaviors are more important than others is by no means new here (e.g., see Dainton, 1998), and conceptual and empirical progress toward delineating frequency versus importance is being made (see Haas, 2001). Building on this presumption that various maintenance mechanisms are differentially important:

It is proposed that differing maintenance mechanisms may be differentially important in LDRs as opposed to geographically close relationships and in obligatory versus voluntary relationships, and may vary in importance among active, latent, and commemorative relationships.

The preceding propositions comport well with Sigman's (1991, 1998) discussion of relational continuity. Sigman took the elegantly simple position that time apart disrupts relational continuity. These gaps in time and space are bridged by "continuity units." Continuity units are defined as "devices to transcend the limitations of co-presence" (Sigman, 1991, p. 109). In other words, relationships are maintained through the enactment of behaviors that construct the continuation of a relationship when individuals are not in each other's presence or not otherwise interacting. These behaviors are engaged in before separation, during separation, and upon reuniting, though it is advanced here that not all relational partners will reunite; nonetheless, their relationship is continued.

Gilbertson, Dindia, and Allen (1998) offered some examples of these continuity units that continue relationships and noted their similarity to many routine maintenance behaviors (Dainton, 1998; Dainton & Stafford, 1993). However, it is proposed here that such units may be routine (unintentional) or strategic (intentional). Strategic or intentional behaviors are those performed with the goal of relational facilitation, whereas routine or unintentional behaviors result in relational maintenance as a by-product (Dainton, 2003; Dainton & Stafford, 1993). Behaviors enacted before separation may include routine simple references to the fact that the relationship will continue when separated, such as the phrase "see you tomorrow" or strategically provide the partner with a physical object to symbolize the relationship. During separation, these artifacts associated with the relationship or partner such as wedding rings, photographs, or a grandparent's scrapbook maintain relational continuity (Gibertson et al., 1998).

Cognitively orienting toward the relationship during absence sustains it as well. Participating in family rituals that call to mind the absent person serves this purpose. When apart, cards or letters may be sent, or behaviors may be interactive such as telephone calls. Interactive media is said to momentarily recreate copresence. These events remind others, and self, of the continuation of the relationship and all that comes with that relationship (Sigman, 1991). Finally, when individuals do reunite, they again recognize the relationship as one that has continued during the time apart. They may use routine greetings, expressions of affection, or filling each other in about events during the absence (Gilbertson et al., 1998).

Sigman's (1991, 1998) perspective is directly concerned with preseparation, absence, and reunification of relational partners, and thus is a logical orientation to consider for the maintenance of LDRs. Given that in the face of decreased interactions, mental representations, such as daydreaming, and individually enacted behaviors, such as looking at photographs, may have increased salience in their role in relational maintenance, the way such behaviors might be routinely or strategically enacted, before, during, and after a separation, and the relative importance of various behaviors in differing relational contexts warrant further consideration.

A final caveat must be offered: Maintenance has been considered as responses to perceptions of inequity enacted to sustain desired relational features. Yet, perhaps these maintenance behaviors not only lead to certain relational qualities but are a result of them. In accordance with equity theory, (in)equity not only influences one's maintenance behaviors and hence one's relational characteristics, it is also a result of them. For example, (dis)satisfaction is both a cause and a result of the maintenance behaviors employed. This causal multidirectional cycle is further explained by Stafford (2003). In short, the possibility remains that maintenance behaviors not only serve to maintain a relationship, they in turn may also be physical, behavioral, and cognitive manifestations of the state of the relationship. However, it is the link between maintenance as a process and maintenance as a state, the mutually recursive process of perceptions of (in)equity, maintenance behaviors and relational definitions, that is intriguing (Stafford, 1994). Thus, a final proposition is offered:

Maintenance mechanisms simultaneously sustain desired relational definitions and are manifestations of relational definitions.

The maintenance behaviors identified in this program (see chap. 3, this volume) have been referred to in various texts as prescriptions for maintaining satisfying relationships. And although individuals report using these behaviors to sustain relationships, causal links remain illusive (Stafford, 2003; cf. Canary, Stafford, & Semic, 2002). Canary and Stafford (2001) have repeatedly offered this caution and have even noted that openness has not always been found to be correlated with positive relational features. Moreover, the delineation of one universal set of features is unlikely. Rather, the quest is to examine which behaviors may sustain which types of relationships under what conditions, and the role equity plays in association with various maintenance mechanisms.

In closing, additional or modified propositions with primary relevance to LDRs and cross-residential relationships are offered:

- In selected relational contexts, forces sustaining desired relational definitions are as strong as, if not more so than, forces tearing away at these definitions.
- Perceptional distortion is a means of relational maintenance.

- Maintenance mechanisms will vary in frequency and importance among relationships that are active, latent, and commemorative.
- Maintenance mechanisms will vary in frequency and importance among relationships that are relatively voluntary verses those that are relatively obligatory.
- Maintenance mechanisms will vary in frequency and importance between LDRs and geographically close relationships.
- Maintenance mechanisms simultaneously sustain desired relational definitions and are manifestations of relational definitions.

In sum, examination of LDRs reveals that maintenance is contingent on a complex interplay of societal structures, expectations, perceptions, memories, interaction, individual internal dispositions or traits, barriers, and various definitions of success.

Epilogue

Two bits of idealistic and unachieved personal philosophy are offered to close this text. First, humans should not be motivated on the basis of their own rewards, or even perceptions of fairness. A model of human interaction transcendent of equity concerns would create a more humane world.

Second, though shared realities and overlapping worldviews may make our personal relationships and our lives significantly easier, more often than not, if we are able to offer unconditional acceptance and tolerance for unshared meanings and worldviews beyond our comprehension, we might be able to maintain our relationships, geographically near and far, more readily as well as develop relationships more worthy of being maintained.

References

Adams, J. (1965). Inequity in social exchange. In L. Berkowitz (Ed.), *Advances in exper-imental social psychology* (Vol. 2, pp. 279–299). New York: Academic Press.

Adams, R. G. (1998). The demise of territorial determinism. In R. G. Adams & G. Allan (Eds.), *Placing friendship in context* (pp. 153–182). Cambridge, England: Cambridge University Press.

Adams, R. G., & Blieszner, R. (1993). Resources for friendship intervention. *Journal of Sociology and Social Welfare, 20*, 159–175.

Afifi, T. D., & Schrodt, P. (2003). "Feeling caught" as a mediator of adolescents' and young adults' avoidance and satisfaction with their parents in divorced and non-divorced households. *Communication Monographs, 70*, 142–173.

Ainsworth, M. D. S., Blehar, M. S., Waters, E., & Wall, S. (1978). *Patterns of attachment: A psychological study of the strange situation.* Hillsdale, NJ: Lawrence Erlbaum Associates.

Aldous, J. (1995). New views of grandparents in intergenerational context. *Journal of Family Issues, 16*, 104–122.

Allan, G. (1977). Sibling solidarity. *Journal of Marriage and the Family, 39*, 177–184.

Allan, G. (1979). *A sociology of friendship and kin.* London: Allen & Unwin.

Allen, K. R., Blieszner, R., & Roberto, K. A. (2000). Families in the middle and later years: A review and critique of research in the 1990s. *Journal of Marriage and the Family, 62*, 911–926.

Amato, P. R. (2000). The consequences of divorce for adults and children. *Journal of Marriage and the Family, 62*, 1269–1287.

Amato, P. R., & Gilbreth, J. G. (1999). Nonresident fathers and children's well-being: A meta-analysis. *Journal of Marriage and the Family, 61*, 557–573.

Amato, P. R., & Rezac, S. J. (1994). Contact with nonresident parents, interparental conflict, and children's behavior. *Journal of Family Issues, 15*, 191–207.

Anderson, E. A. (1992). Decision-making style: Impact on satisfaction of the commuter couples' lifestyle. *Journal of Family and Economic Issues, 13*, 5–21.

Anderson, E. A., & Spruill, J. W. (1993). The dual-career commuter family: A lifestyle on the move. *Marriage and Family Review, 19*, 131–147.

Angrist, J. D., & Johnson, J. H. (2000). Effects of work-related absences on families: Evidence from the Gulf War. *Industrial and Labor Relations Review, 54*, 41–58.

Applewhite, L. W., Jr., & Mays, R. A. (1996). Parent–child separation: A comparison of maternally and paternally separated children in military families. *Child Adolescent Social Work Journal, 13*, 23–39.

Arditti, J., Lambert-Shute, J., & Joest, K. (2003). Saturday morning at the jail: implications of incarceration for families and children. *Family Relations, 52*, 195–204.

Arendell, T. (1997). The new father. In T. Arendell (Ed.), *Contemporary parenting: Challenges and issues* (pp. 154–195). Thousand Oaks, CA: Sage.

Astin, H. S., & Milem, J. F. (1997). The status of academic couples in U.S. institutions. In M. A. Ferber & J. W. Loeb (Eds.), *Academic couples: Problems and promise* (pp. 128–155). Champaign: University of Illinois Press.

Aylor, D. (2003). Maintaining long-distance relationships. In D. J. Canary & M. Dainton (Eds.), *Maintaining relationships through communication: Relational, contextual, and cultural variations* (pp. 127–140). Mahwah, NJ: Lawrence Erlbaum Associates.

Bahg, C. G. (1990). Major system theories throughout the world. *Behavioral Science, 35*, 79–107.

Baker, A. (2002). What makes an online relationship successful: Clues from couples who met in cyberspace. *CyberPsychology and Behavior, 5*, 363–376.

Baldock, C. V. (2000). Migrant and their parents: Caring from a distance. *Journal of Family Issues, 21*, 205–224.

Bank, S. P., & Kahn, M. D. (1997). *The sibling bond.* New York: Basic Books.

Baxter, L. A., & Montgomery, B. M. (1996). *Relating: Dialogues and dialects.* New York: Guilford.

Baym, N. K. (2002). Interpersonal life online. In L. Lievrouw & S. Livingstone (Eds.), *Handbook of new media: Social shaping and consequences of ICTs* (pp. 62–76). Thousand Oaks, CA: Sage.

Beckerman, A. (1994). Mothers in prison: Meeting the prerequisite conditions for permanency planning. *Social Work, 39*, 9–14.

Bedford, V. H. (1996). Relationships between adult siblings. In A. E. Auhagen & M. von Salisch (Eds.), *The diversity of human relationships* (pp. 120–140). New York: Cambridge University Press.

Bedford, V. H., & Blieszner, R. (2000). Personal relationships in later life families. In R. M. Milardo & S. W. Duck (Eds.), *Families as relationships* (pp. 157–174). Chichester, England: Wiley.

Bell, D. B., Bartone, J., Bartone, P. T., Schumm, W. R., & Gade, P. A. (1997). *USAREUR family support during Operation Joint Endeavor: A summary report.* Alexandria, VA: U.S. Army Research Institute for the Behavioral and Social Science.

Bell, D. B., & Schumm, W. R. (1999). Family adaptation to deployments. In I. P. McClure (Ed.), *Pathways to the future: A review of military family research* (pp. 109–131). Scranton, PA: Military Family Institute.

Bell, D. B., & Schumm, W. R. (2000). Providing family support during military deployments. In J. A. Martin, L. N. Rosen, & L. R. Sparacino (Eds.), *The military family: A practice guide for human service providers* (pp. 139–152). Westport, CT: Praeger.

Bengston, V. L. (2001). Beyond the nuclear family: The increasing importance of multigenerational bonds. *Journal of Marriage and the Family, 63*, 1–16.

Bengston, V. L., & Roberts, R. E. L. (1991). Intergenerational solidarity in aging families: An example of formal theory construction. *Journal of Marriage and the Family, 53*, 856–870.

Berger, P. L., & Kellner, H. (1964). Marriage and the construction of reality. *Diogenes, 64*, 1–4.

Berger, P. L., & Luckmann, T. (1966). *The social construction of reality: A treatise in the sociology of knowledge*. Garden City, NY: Doubleday.

Berscheid, E., Snyder, M., & Omoto, A. M. (1989). The relationship closeness inventory: Assessing the closeness of interpersonal relationships. *Journal of Personality and Social Psychology, 57*, 792–807.

Binstock, G., & Thornton, A. (2003). Separations, reconciliations, and living apart in cohabitating and marital unions. *Journal of Marriage and Family, 65*, 432–473.

Black, W. (1993). Military-induced family separation: A stress reduction intervention. *Social Work, 38*, 273–280.

Blau, P. (1964). *Exchange and power in social life*. New York: Wiley.

Blieszner, R., & Adams, R. G. (1992). *Adult friendships*. Thousand Oaks, CA: Sage.

Blumer, H. (1969). *Symbolic interactionism*. Englewood Cliffs, NJ: Prentice Hall.

Blumer, H., & Katz, E. (1974). *The uses of mass communications*. Thousand Oaks, CA: Sage.

Bochner, A. P. (1982). On the efficacy of openness in close relationships. In M. Burgoon (Ed.), *Communication yearbook* (Vol. 2, pp. 109–124). New Brunswick, NJ: Transaction Press.

Bochner, A. P. (1984). The functions of human communication in interpersonal bonding. In C. C. Arnold & J. W. Bowers (Eds.), *Handbook of rhetorical and communication theory* (pp. 544–621). Newton, MA: Allyn & Bacon.

Bochner, A.P., & Eisenberg, E. M. (1987). Family process: Systems perspectives. In C. Berger & S. Chaffee (Eds.), *Handbook of communication science* (pp. 544–566). Beverly Hills, CA: Sage.

Boon, S. D., & Brussoni, M. J. (1996). Young adults' relationships with their "closest" grandparents. *Journal of Social Behavior & Personality, 11*, 439–458.

Boss, P., McCubbin, H. I., & Lester, G. (1979). The corporate executive wife's coping patterns in response to routine husband-father absence: Implications for family stress theory. *Family Process, 18*, 79–86.

Bowlby, J. (1973). *Attachment and loss: Vol.2. Separation: Anxiety and anger*. New York: Basic Books.

Brannen, J., Heptinstall, E., & Bhopal, K. (2000). *Connecting children: Care and family life in later childhood*. London: Routledge Falmer.

Braver, S. L., & O'Connell, D. (1998). *Divorced dads: Shattering the myths*. New York: Tarcher.

Brenner, E. (2001). *Fathers in prison: A review of the data*. Philadelphia: National Center on Fathers and Families.

Bronfenbrenner, U. (1979). *The ecology of human development: Experiments by nature and by design*. Cambridge, MA: Harvard University Press.

Brooks, M. K. (1993). *How can I help? Working with children of incarcerated parents*. New York: Osborne.

Buchanan, C. M. (2000). Adolescents' adjustment to divorce. In R. D. Taylor & M. C. Wang (Eds.), *Resilience across contexts: Family, work, culture, and community* (pp. 180–216). Mahwah, NJ: Lawrence Erlbaum Associates.

Buchanan, C. M., & Heiges, K. L. (2001). When conflict continues after the marriage ends: Effects of post-divorce conflict on children. In J. H. Grych & F. D. Fincham (Eds.), *Interparental conflict and child development* (pp. 337–362). Cambridge, England: Cambridge University Press.

Buchanan, C. M., Maccoby, E. E., & Dornbusch, S. M. (1996). *Adolescents after divorce*. Cambridge, MA: Harvard University Press.

Bunker, B. B., Zubek, J. M., Vanderslice, V. A., & Rice, R. W. (1992). Quality of life in dual-career families: Commuting versus single-residence couples. *Journal of Marriage and Family, 54*, 339–407.

Bureau of Justice Statistics. (2003). *Key facts at a glance: Correctional populations*. Washington, DC: U.S. Department of Justice.

Burgess, E. W. (1926). The family as a unit of interacting personalities. *The Family, 7*, 3–9.

Burgess, E. W., Locke, H. J., & Thomes, M. M. (1971). *The family: From traditional to companionship* (4th ed.). New York: Van Nostrand Reinhold.

Campbell, C. L., & Demi, A. S. (2000). Adult children of fathers missing in action (MIA): An examination of emotional distress, grief, and family hardiness. *Family Relations, 49*, 267–275.

Canary, D. J., & Dainton, M. (Eds.). (2003). *Maintaining relationships through communication*. Mahwah, NJ: Lawrence Erlbaum Associates.

Canary, D. J., & Stafford, L. (1992). Relational maintenance strategies and equity in marriage. *Communication Monographs, 59*, 243–267.

Canary, D. J., & Stafford, L. (1993). Preservation of relational characteristics: Maintenance of strategies, equity, and locus of control. In P. J. Kalbfleisch (Ed.), *Interpersonal communication: Evolving interpersonal relationships* (pp. 237–259). Hillsdale, NJ: Lawrence Erlbaum Associates.

Canary, D. J., & Stafford, L. (Eds.). (1994a). *Communication and relational maintenance*. San Diego, CA: Academic Press.

Canary, D. J., & Stafford, L. (1994b). Maintaining relationships through strategic and routine interaction. In D. J. Canary & L. Stafford (Eds.), *Communication and relational maintenance* (pp. 3–22). San Diego, CA: Academic Press.

Canary, D. J., & Stafford, L. (2001). Equity in the preservation of personal relationships. In J. Harvey & A. Wenzel (Eds.), *Close romantic relationships: Preservation and enhancement* (pp. 133–151). Mahwah, NJ: Lawrence Erlbaum Associates.

Canary, D. J., Stafford, L., Hause, K., & Wallace, L. (1993). An inductive analysis of relational maintenance strategies: A comparison among lovers, relatives, friends, and others. *Communication Research Reports, 10*, 5–14.

Canary, D. J., Stafford, L., & Semic, B. A. (2002). A panel study of the associations between maintenance strategies and relational characteristics. *Journal of Marriage and the Family, 64*, 395–406.

Canary, D. J., & Zelley, E. D. (2000). Current research programs in relational maintenance. In M. E. Roloff (Ed.), *Communication yearbook 23* (pp. 305–339). Thousand Oaks, CA: Sage.

Cantor, M. (1979). Neighbors and friends. *Research on Aging, 1*, 434–463.

Carlson, E., & Carlson, R. (2002). *Navy marriages and deployments* (Rev ed.). New York: University of American Press.

Carpenter, D., & Knox, D. (1986). Relationship maintenance of college students separated during courtship. *College Student Journal, 20*, 86–88.

Carter, B., & McGoldrick, M. (Eds.). (1999). *The expanded family life cycle* (3rd ed.). Boston: Allyn & Bacon.

Cassidy, J., & Shaver, P. R. (Eds.). (2002). *Handbook of attachment: Theory, research, and clinical applications*. New York: Guilford.

Cate, R. M., Levin, L. A., & Richmond, L. S. (2002). Premarital relationship stability: A review of recent research. *Journal of Social and Personal Relationships, 19*, 261–284.

Cate, R. M., & Lloyd, S. A. (1992). *Courtship*. Newbury Park, CA: Sage.

Charon, J. M. (2004). *Symbolic interactionism: An introduction, an interpretation, an integration* (8th ed.). Upper Saddle River, NJ: Prentice Hall.

Cherlin, A., & Furstenberg, F. F. (1985). Styles and strategies of grandparenting. In V. L. L. Bengston & J. F. Robertson (Eds.), *Grandparenthood* (pp. 97–116). Beverly Hills, CA: Sage.

Cicirelli, V. G. (1991). Sibling relationships in adulthood. In S. K. Pfeifer & M. B. Sussman (Eds.), *Families: Intergenerational and generational connections* (pp. 291–309). New York: Hayworth.

Cicirelli, V. G. (1995). *Sibling relationships across the life span*. New York: Plenum.

Cicirelli, V. G. (1996). Sibling relationships in middle and old age. In G. Brody (Ed.), *Sibling relationships: Their causes and consequences* (pp. 47–73). Norwood, NJ: Ablex.

Cicirelli, V. G., Coward, R. T., & Dwyer, J. W. (1992). Siblings as caregivers for impaired elders. *Research on Aging, 14*, 331–350.

Cicirelli, V. G., & Nussbaum, J. F. (1989). Relationships with siblings in later life. In J. F. Nussbaum (Ed.), *Life-span communication: Normative processes* (pp. 283–299). Mahwah, NJ: Lawrence Erlbaum Associates.

Cimo, J. (1992). *Distant parents*. Brunswick, NJ: Rutgers University Press.

Conville, R. L., & Rogers, L. E. (Eds.). (1998). *The meaning of "relationship" in interpersonal communication*. Westport, CT: Praeger.

Cooksey, E. C., & Craig, P. H. (1998). Parenting from a distance: The effects of paternal characteristics on contact between nonresidential fathers and children. *Demography, 35,* 187–200.

Cooney, T. M. (1997). Parent–child relationships across adulthood. In S. W. Duck (Ed.), *Handbook of personal relationships* (pp. 451–468). New York: Wiley.

Cooney, T. M. (2000). Parent–child relations across adulthood. In R. M. Milardo & S. W. Duck (Eds.), *Families as relationships* (pp. 39–58). Chichester, England: Wiley.

Cornwell, B., & Lundgren, D. (2001). Love on the Internet: Involvement and misrepresentation in romantic relationships in cyberspace vs. real space. *Computers in Human Behavior, 17,* 197–211.

Creasey, G. L., & Kaliher, G. (1994). Age differences in grandchildren's perceptions of relations with grandparents. *Journal of Adolescence, 17,* 411–426.

Crosnoe, R. (2000). Friendships in childhood and adolescence: The life course and new directions. *Social Psychology Quarterly, 63,* 377–391.

Cutrona, C. E. (1996). *Social support in couples: Marriages as a resource in times of need.* Thousand Oaks, CA: Sage.

Daft, R. L., & Lengel, R. H. (1984). Information richness: A new approach to managerial behavior and organization design. In B. M. Straw & L. L. Cummings (Eds.), *Research in organizational behavior* (Vol. 6, pp. 191–233). Greenwich, CT: JAI.

Daft, R. L., & Lengel, R. H. (1986). Organizational information requirements, media richness and structural design. *Management Science, 32,* 554–571.

Dainton, M. (1998). Everyday interaction in marital relationships: Variations in relative importance and event duration. *Communication Reports, 11,* 101–110.

Dainton, M. (2003). Framing the maintenance of relationships through communication. In D. J. Canary and M. Dainton (Eds.), *Maintaining relationships through communication* (pp. 299–321). Mahwah, NJ: Lawrence Erlbaum Associates.

Dainton, M., & Aylor, B. (2001). A relational uncertainty analysis of jealousy, trust, and maintenance in long-distance versus geographically close relationships. *Communication Quarterly, 49,* 172–188.

Dainton, M., & Aylor, B. (2002). Patterns of communication channel use in the maintenance of long-distance relationships. *Communication Research Reports, 19,* 118–129.

Dainton, M., & Stafford, L. (1993). Routine maintenance behaviors: A comparison of relationship type, partner similarity, and sex differences. *Journal of Social and Personal Relationships, 10,* 255–272.

DaVanzo, J., & Rahman, M. O. (1993). American families: Trends and correlates. *Population Index, 59,* 350–386.

Davidson, N. (1990). Life without father: America's greatest social catastrophe. *Policy Review, 51,* 40–44.

Davis, M. S. (1973). *Intimate relationships.* New York: Free Press.

Defense Manpower Data Center. (1999). *Effective strategies to assist spouses of junior enlisted members with employment.* Alexandria, VA: Survey and Program Evaluation Division.

DeFrain, J., & Olson, D. H. (1999). Contemporary family patterns and relationships. In M. B. Sussman, S. Steinmetz, & G. Peterson (Eds.), *Handbook of marriage and the family* (2nd ed., pp. 309–326). New York: Plenum.

Dellmann-Jenkins, M., Bernard-Paolucci, T. S., & Rushing, B. (1994). Does distance make the heart grow fonder? A comparison of college students in long-distance and geographically-close dating relationships. *College Student Journal, 28*, 212–219.

Dewit, D. J., Wister, A., & Burch, T. K. (1988). Physical distance and social contact between elders and their adult children. *Research on Aging, 10*, 56–80.

Diggs, R. C., & Stafford, L. (1998). Maintaining marital relationships: A comparison between African American and European American married individuals. In V. J. Duncan (Ed.), *Towards achieving MAAT* (pp. 192–292). Dubuque, IA: Kendall/Hunt.

Dimmick, J., Kline, S., & Stafford, L. (2000). The gratification niches of personal e-mail and the telephone: Competition, displacement, and complementarity. *Communication Research, 27*, 227–248.

Dimmick, J., Sikand, J., & Patterson, S. (1994). The gratifications of the household telephone: Sociability, instrumentality and reassurance. *Communication Research, 21*, 643–663.

Dindia, K. (1994). A multiphasic view of relationship maintenance strategies. In D. J. Canary & L. Stafford (Eds.), *Communication and relational maintenance* (pp. 91–112). San Diego, CA: Academic Press.

Dindia, K., & Baxter, L. A. (1987). Strategies for repairing and maintaining marital relationships. *Journal of Social and Personal Relationships, 4*, 143–158.

Dindia, K., & Canary, D. J. (1993). Definitions and theoretical perspectives on maintaining relationships. *Journal of Social and Personal Relationships, 10*, 163–173.

Douvan, E., & Pleck, J. (1978). Separation as support. In R. Rapoport & R. Rapoport (Eds.), *Working couples* (pp. 138–146). New York: Harper & Row.

Downs, V. C. (1989). The grandparent–grandchild relationship. In J. F. Nussbaum (Ed.), *Life-span communication: Normative processes* (pp. 257–281). Hillsdale, NJ: Lawrence Erlbaum Associates.

Drummet, A. R., Coleman, M., & Cable, S. (2003). Military families under stress: Implications for family life education. *Family Relations, 52*, 279–287.

Dubas, J. S., & Peterson, A. C. (1996). Geographical distance from parents and adjustment during adolescence and young adulthood. *New Directions for Child Development, 71*, 3–19.

Duck, S. W. (1988). *Relating to others.* Chicago: Dorsey.

Duck, S. W. (1990). Where do all the kisses go? Rapport, positivity and relational level of analysis of interpersonal enmeshment. *Psychological Inquiry, 1*, 47–53.

Duck, S. W. (1994a). *Meaningful relationships: Talking, sense, and relating.* Thousand Oaks, CA: Sage.

Duck, S. W. (1994b). Steady s(he) goes: Relational maintenance as a shared meaning system. In D. J. Canary & L. Stafford (Eds.), *Communication and relational maintenance* (pp. 45–60). San Diego, CA: Academic Press.

Duck, S. W., Acitelli, L. K., & Nicholson, J. H. (2000). Family life as an experimental quilt. In R. M. Milardo & S. W. Duck (Eds.), *Families as relationships* (pp. 175–189). Chichester, England: Wiley.

Duck, S. W., & Pittman, G. (1994). Social and personal relationships. In M. L. Knapp & G. R. Miller (Eds.), *Handbook of interpersonal communication* (2nd ed., pp. 676–695). Thousand Oaks, CA: Sage.

Duck, S. W., Rutt, D. J., Hurst, M. H., & Strejc, H. (1991). Some evident truths about everyday conversation: All communications are not created equal. *Human Communication Research, 18,* 228–267.

Dudley, J. R. (1991). Increasing our understanding of divorced fathers who have infrequent contact with their children. *Family Relations, 40,* 279–285.

Dunham, C. C. (1995). A link between generations: Intergenerational relations and depression in aging parents. *Journal of Family Issues, 16,* 450–465.

Egan, J. (2003, November 23). Love in the time of no time. *New York Times,* p. 66.

Elder, G. H., Jr., & Clipp, E. C. (1988). Wartime losses and social bonding: Influences across 40 years in men's lives. *Psychiatry, 51,* 177–198.

Emery, R. E. (1994). *Renegotiating family relationships: Divorce, child custody, and mediation.* New York: Guilford.

Farris, A. (1978). Commuting. In R. Rapoport & R. Rapoport (Eds.), *Working couples* (pp. 100–107). London: Routledge & Kegan Paul.

Fehr, B. (1996). *Friendship processes.* Thousand Oaks, CA: Sage.

Felmlee, D. H. (2001). No couple is an island: A social network perspective on dyadic stability. *Social Forces, 79,* 1259–1287.

Fields, J. (2003). *Children's living arrangements and characteristics: March 2002.* Washington, DC: U.S. Census Bureau.

Fields, J., & Casper, L. M. (2001). *America's families and living arrangements: March 2000.* Washington, DC: U.S. Census Bureau.

Fields, J. M., Smith, K., Bass, L. E., & Lugaila, T. (2001). *A child's day: Home, school, and play (selected indicators of child well-being).* Washington, DC: U.S. Census Bureau.

Finn, J., & Banach, M. (2000). Victimization online: The downside of seeking human services for women on the Internet. *CyberPsychology & Behavior, 3,* 785–796.

Fischer, C. (1994). *America calling: A social history of the telephone to 1940.* Berkeley: University of California Press.

Fischer, C. S., & Carroll, G. R. (1988). Telephone and automobile diffusion in the United States, 1902–1937. *American Journal of Sociology, 93,* 1153–1178.

Fishman, L. T. (1990). *Women at the wall: A study of prisoners' wives doing time on the outside.* Albany: State University of New York Press.

Fiske, D. W., & Shweder, R. A. (Eds.). (1986). *Metatheory in social science: Pluralisms and subjectivities.* Chicago: University of Chicago Press.

Fitzpatrick, M. A., & Caughlin, J. P. (2002). Interpersonal communication in family relationships. In M. L. Knapp & J. A. Daly (Eds.), *The handbook of interpersonal communication* (3rd ed., pp. 726–777). Thousand Oaks, CA: Sage.

Forsyth, C. J., & Gramling, R. (1987). Feast or famine: Alternative management techniques among periodic-father absence single career families. *International Journal of Sociology of the Family, 17*, 183–196.

Frost-Knappman, E., & Cullen-Dupont, K. (Eds.). (1997). *Women's rights on trial: 101 historic trials from Anne Hutchinson to the Virginia Military Institute cadets*. Detroit, MI: Gale.

Fulmer, R. (1999). Becoming an adult: Leaving home and staying connected. In B. Carter & M. McGoldrick (Eds.), *The expanded family life cycle* (pp. 215–230). Boston: Allyn & Bacon.

Furstenberg, F. F., Jr., & Nord, C. W. (1985). Parenting apart: Patterns of child-rearing after marital disruption. *Journal of Marriage and the Family, 47*, 893–904.

Gabbard, S., Mines, R., & Boccalandro, B. (1994). *Migrant farmworkers: Pursuing security in an unstable labor market*. Washington, DC: U.S. Department of Labor, Office of the Assistant Secretary for Policy.

Gabel, S. (1992). Children of incarcerated and criminal parents: Adjustment, behavior, and prognosis. *Bulletin of the American Academy of Psychiatry Law, 20*, 33–45.

Ganong, L., Coleman, M., & Weaver, S. (2002). Relationship maintenance and enhancement in stepfamilies: Clinical applications. In J. H. Harvey & A. Wenzel (Eds.), *Maintaining and enhancing close relationships: Linking theory with practice* (pp. 105–132). Mahwah, NJ: Lawrence Erlbaum Associates.

Gergen, K. J. (1991). *The saturated self: Dilemmas of identity in contemporary life*. New York: Basic Books.

Gerstel, N. (1978). The feasibility of commuter marriage. In P. J. Stein, J. Richman, & N. Hannon (Eds.), *The family: Functions, conflicts, and symbols* (pp. 357–367). Reading, MA: Addison-Wesley.

Gerstel, N. (1979). Marital alternatives and the regulation of sex: Commuter couples as a test case. *Alternative Lifestyles, 2*, 145–176.

Gerstel, N., & Gross, H. (1982). Commuter marriages: A review. *Marriage and Family Review, 5*, 71–93.

Gerstel, N., & Gross, H. (1983). Commuter marriage: Couples who live apart. In E. D. Macklin & R. H. Rubin (Eds.), *Contemporary families and alternative lifestyles* (pp. 180–193). Beverly Hills, CA: Sage.

Gerstel, N., & Gross, H. (1984). *Commuter marriage: A study of work and family*. New York: Guilford.

Gerstel, N., & Gross, H. (1987). Commuter marriage: A microcosm of career and family conflict. In N. Gerstel & H. Gross (Eds.), *Families and work* (pp. 422–433). Philadelphia: Temple University Press.

Giarrusso, R., Stallings, M., & Bengston, V. L. L. (1995). The "intergenerational stake" hypothesis revisited: Parent–child differences in perceptions of relationships 20 years later. In V. L. L. Bengston, K. W. Schaie, & L. M. Burton (Eds.), *Adult intergenerational relations: Effects of societal change* (pp. 227–263). New York: Springer.

Gilbertson, J., Dindia, K., & Allen, M. (1998). Relational continuity, constructional units and the maintenance of relationships. *Journal of Social and Personal Relationships, 15*, 774–790.

Giles, D. C. (2002). Parasocial interaction: A review of the literature and a model for future research. *Media Psychology, 4*, 279–305.

Gimbel, C., & Booth, A. (1994). Why does military combat experience adversely affect marital relations? *Journal of Marriage and Family, 56*, 691–703.

Goffman, E. (1959). *The presentation of self in everyday life*: Garden City, NY: Doubleday Anchor.

Goffman, E. (1983). The interaction order. *American Sociological Review, 48*, 1–17.

Golish, T. (2000). Changes in closeness between adult children and their parents: A turning point analysis. *Communication Reports, 13*, 79–97.

Golum Quddus, A. H. (1992). The adjustment of couples who live apart: The case of Bangladesh. *Journal of Comparative Family Studies, 23*, 285–294.

Goodwin, S. A., Fiske, S. T., Rosen, L. D., & Rosenthal, A. M. (2002). The eye of the beholder: Romantic goals and impression biases. *Journal of Experimental Social Psychology, 38*, 232–241.

Gottman, J. M. (1979). *Marital interaction: Experimental investigations*. New York: Academic Press.

Gottman, J. M. (1994). *What predicts divorce: The relationship between marital processes and marital outcomes*. Hillsdale, NJ: Lawrence Erlbaum Associates.

Gottman, J. M., Coan, J., Carrere, S., & Swanson, C. (1998). Predicting marital happiness and stability from newlywed interactions. *Journal of Marriage & the Family, 60*, 193–201.

Gottman, J. M., & Krokoff, L. J. (1989). Marital interaction and satisfaction: A longitudinal view. *Journal of Consulting and Clinical Psychology, 57*, 47–52.

Gottman, J. M., & Levenson, R. W. (2002). A two-factor model for predicting when a couple will divorce: Exploratory analyses using 14-year longitudinal data. *Family Process, 41*, 83–96.

Govaerts, K., & Dixon, D. N. (1988). Until careers do us part: Vocational and marital satisfaction in the dual-career commuter marriage. *International Journal for Advanced Counseling, 11*, 265–281.

Graber, J. A., & Brooks-Gunn, J. (1996). Transitions and turning points: Navigating the passage from childhood through adolescence. *Developmental Psychology, 32*, 768–776.

Granovetter, M. (1983). The strength of weak ties: A network theory revisited. *Sociological Theory, 1*, 201–233.

Gratton, B., & Haber, C. (1993). In search of "intimacy at a distance": Family history from the perspective of elderly women. *Journal of Aging Studies, 7*, 183–194.

Griswold, R L. (1993). *Fatherhood in America: A history*. New York: Basic Books.

Gross, H. (1980). Dual-career couples who live apart: Two types. *Journal of Marriage and the Family, 42*, 567–576.

Groves, M. M., & Horm-Wingerd, D. M. (1991). Commuter marriages: Personal, family, and career issues. *Sociology and Social Research, 75*, 212–217.

Grych, J. H., & Fincham, F. D. (1990). Marital conflict and children's adjustment: A cognitive contextual framework. *Psychological Bulletin, 108*, 267–290.

Guldner, G. T. (1992). *Propinquity and dating relationships: Toward a theory of long-distance romantic relationships including an exploratory study of college students' relationships-at-a-distance.* Unpublished manuscript, West Lafayette, IN.

Guldner, G. T. (1996). Long-distance romantic relationships: Prevalence and separation-related symptoms in college students. *Journal of College Student Development, 37,* 289–296.

Guldner, G. T. (2001). Long-distance relationships and emergency medicine residency. *Annals of Emergency Medicine, 37,* 103–106.

Guldner, G. T., & Swensen, C. H. (1995). Time spent together and relationship quality: Long-distance relationships as a test case. *Journal of Social and Personal Relationships, 12,* 313–320.

Gunn, D., & Gunn, C. (2000, September). *The quality of electronically maintained relationships.* Paper presented at the Association of Internet Researchers, Lawrence, KS.

Haas, S. M. (2001, November). *Frequency versus importance of relational maintenance behaviors.* Paper presented at the National Communication Association, Chicago.

Haas, S. M., & Stafford, L. (1998). An initial examination of maintenance behaviors in gay and lesbian relationships. *Journal of Social and Personal Relationships, 15,* 846–855.

Hairston, C. F. (1991). Family ties during imprisonment: Important to whom and for what? *Journal of Sociology and Social Welfare, 18,* 87–104.

Hairston, C. F. (2001a). Fathers in prison: Responsible fatherhood and responsible public policy. *Marriage and Family Review, 32,* 111–135.

Hairston, C. F. (2001b). The forgotten parent: Understanding the forces that influence incarcerated fathers' relationships with their children. In C. Seymour & C. Hairston (Eds.), *Children with parents in prison: Child welfare, policy, programs, and practice issues* (pp. 149–171). New Brunswick, NJ: Transaction Press.

Harvey, J. H., & Wenzel, A. (Eds.). (2001). *Close romantic relationships: Maintenance and enhancement.* Mahwah, NJ: Lawrence Erlbaum Associates.

Harvey, J. H., & Wenzel, A. (Eds.). (2002). *A clinician's guide to maintaining and enhancing close relationships.* Mahwah, NJ: Lawrence Erlbaum Associates.

Harwood, J. (2000a). Communication media use in the grandparent–grandchild relationship. *Journal of Communication, 50,* 56–78.

Harwood, J. (2000b). Communicative predictors of solidarity in the grandparent–grandchild relationship. *Journal of Social and Personal Relationships, 17,* 743–766.

Harwood, J. (2001). Comparing grandchildren's and grandparent's stake in their relationship. *International Journal of Aging and Human Development, 53,* 195–210.

Harwood, J., & Lin, M.-C. (2000). Affiliation, pride, exchange, and distance in grandparent's accounts of relationships with their college-aged grandchildren. *Journal of Communication, 50,* 32–47.

Harwood, J., McKee, J., & Lin, M.-C. (2000). Younger and older adults' schematic representations of intergenerational communication. *Communication Monographs, 67,* 20–41.

Hatfield, E., Traupmann, J., Sprecher, S., Utne, M., & Hay, J. (1985). Equity and intimate relationships: Recent research. In W. Ickes (Ed.), *Compatible and incompatible relationships* (pp. 91–117). New York: Springer-Verlag.

Hawkins, M. W., Carrere, S., & Gottman, J. M. (2002). Marital sentiment override: Does it influence couples' perceptions? *Journal of Marriage & the Family, 64,* 193–201.

Heider, F. (1958). *The psychology of interpersonal relations.* New York: Wiley.

Helgeson, V. S. (1994). Long-distance romantic relationships: Sex differences in adjustment and breakup. *Personality and Social Psychology Bulletin, 20,* 245–256.

Hendrick, C., & Hendrick, S. S. (1988). Lovers wear rose colored glasses. *Journal of Social and Personal Relationships, 5,* 161–183.

Hernandez, M., & McGoldrick, M. (1999). Migration and the family life cycle. In B. Carter & M. McGoldrick (Eds.), *The expanded life cycle* (3rd ed., pp. 169–184). Boston: Allyn & Bacon.

Hess, J. A. (2003). Maintaining undesired relationships. In M. Dainton & D. J. Canary (Eds.), *Maintaining relationships through communication* (pp. 103–126). Mahwah, NJ: Lawrence Erlbaum Associates.

Hetherington, E. M., Cox, M., & Cox, R. (1982). Effects of divorce on parents and children. In M. E. Lamb (Ed.), *Nontraditional families* (pp. 233–288). Hillsdale, NJ: Lawrence Erlbaum Associates.

Hetherington, E. M., & Stanley-Hagen, M. (1997). The effects of divorce on fathers and their children. In M. E. Lamb (Ed.), *The role of fathers in child development* (pp. 191–244). New York: Wiley.

Hiew, C. C. (1992). Separated by their work: Families with fathers living apart. *Environment and Behavior, 24,* 206–225.

Hill, C. T., Rubin, Z., & Peplau, L. (1976). Breakups before marriage: The end of 103 affairs. *Journal of Social Issues, 32,* 147–168.

Hill, R. (1945). The returning father and his family. *Marriage and Family Living, 7,* 31–34.

Hill, R. (1949). *Families under stress: Adjustment to the crises of war separation and reunion.* New York: Harper.

Hill, R. (1958). Social stresses on the family: Generic features of families under stress. *Social Casework, 39,* 139–150.

Hinde, R. A., & Stevenson-Hinde, J. (Eds.). (1987). *Relationships within families: Mutual influences.* New York: Oxford University Press.

Holladay, S., Denton, D., Harding, D., Lee, M., Lackovich, R., & Coleman, M. (1997). Granddaughters' accounts of the influence of parental mediation on relational closeness with maternal grandmothers. *International Journal of Aging and Human Development, 45,* 23–38.

Holmes, J. G. (2000). Social relationships: The nature and function of relational schemas. *European Journal of Social Psychology, 30,* 447–495.

Holt, P. A., & Stone, G. L. (1988). Needs, coping strategies, and coping outcomes associated with long-distance relationships. *Journal of College Student Development, 29,* 136–141.

Honeycutt, J. M. (2003). *Imagined interactions: Daydreaming about communication.* Cresskill, NJ: Hampton Press.

Honeycutt, J. M., & Cantrill, J. G. (2001). *Cognition, communication, and romantic relationships.* Mahwah, NJ: Lawrence Erlbaum Associates.

Huang, G. G. (2002). *What federal statistics reveal about migrant farmworkers: A summary for education.* Charleston, WV: ERIC Clearinghouse on Rural Education and Small Schools. (ERIC Document Reproduction Service No. ED471487).

Huges, R., Jr., & Hans, J. D. (2001). Computers, the Internet and families: A review of the role new technology plays in family life. *Journal of Family Issues, 22,* 778–792.

Hummert, M. L., & Nussbaum, J. F. (2001). *Aging communication and health: Multidisciplinary perspectives.* Mahwah, NJ: Lawrence Erlbaum Associates.

Hunter, E. J. (1982). *Families under the flag: A review of military family literature.* New York: Praeger.

Ickes, W., & Simpson, J. A. (1997). Managing empathic accuracy in close relationships. In W. Ickes (Ed.), *Empathetic accuracy* (pp. 218–250). New York: Guilford.

Imber-Black, E., & Roberts, J. (1992). *Rituals for our times: Celebrating, healing, and changing our lives and our relationships.* New York: HarperCollins.

Isay, R. (1968). The submariners' wives syndrome. *Psychiatric Quarterly, 42,* 647–652.

Jackson, A. P., Brown, R. P., & Patterson-Stewart, K. E. (2000). African Americans in dual-career commuter marriages: An investigation of their experiences. *The Family Journal, 8,* 22–36.

Jacobs, E. W., & Hicks, M. W. (1987). Periodic family separation: The importance of beliefs in determining outcomes. *Military Family, 7*(2), 3–5.

Johnson, A. J. (2001). Examining the maintenance of friendships: Are there differences between geographically close and long-distance friends? *Communication Quarterly, 49,* 424–435.

Johnson, A. J., Becker, J., Wigley, S., Wittenberg, E., & Haigh, M. (2003, May). *What geographic distance can illustrate about relational closeness: Close long-distance friendships.* Paper presented at the International Communication Association, San Diego, CA.

Johnson, C. L. (2000). Kinship and gender. In D. H. Demo, K. R. Allen, & M. A. Fine (Eds.), *Handbook of family diversity* (pp. 128–148). New York: Oxford University Press.

Johnson, E. J. (1987). Weaving the threads: Equalizing professional and personal demands faced by commuting career couples. *Journal of the National Association of Women Deans and Counselors, 50*(2), 3–10.

Jones, J. M. (2001). *Almost all e-mail users say internet e-mail have made lives better.* Retrieved June 20, 2004, from http://www.gallup.com/content/login.aspx?ci=4711.

Kantor, D., & Lehr, W. (1975). *Inside the family: Toward a theory of family process.* San Francisco: Jossey-Bass.

Kaufman, G., & Uhlenberg, P. (1998). Effects of life course transitions on the quality of relationships between adult children and their parents. *Journal of Marriage & the Family, 60,* 924–928.

Kelley, H. H., & Thibaut, J. W. (1978). *Interpersonal relations: A theory of interdependence.* New York: Wiley.

Kelley, M. L., Herzog-Simmer, P. A., & Harris, M. A. (1994). Effects of military-induced separation on the parenting stress and family functioning of deploying mothers. *Military Psychology, 6,* 125–138.

Kelley, M. L., Hock, E., Smith, K. M., Jarvis, B. S., Bonney, J. F., & Gaffney, M. A. (2001). Internalizing and externalizing behavior of children with enlisted navy mothers experiencing military-induced separation. *Journal of the American Academy of Child and Adolescent Psychiatry, 40,* 464–471.

Kelly, J. B. (1993). Current research on children's post-divorce adjustment. *Family and Conciliation Courts Review, 31,* 29–49.

Kelly, J. B. (2000). Children's adjustment in conflicted marriage and divorce: A decade review of research. *Journal of the American Academy of Child and Adolescent Psychiatry, 39,* 963–973.

Kenny, D. A. (1988). Interpersonal perception: A social relations analysis. *Journal of Social and Personal Relationships, 5,* 247–261.

Kenny, M. E., & Donaldson, G. A. (1991). Contributions of parental attachment and family structure to the social and psychological functioning of first-year college students. *Journal of Counseling Psychology, 38,* 479–486.

King, V., Harris, K. M., & Heard, H. E. (2004). Racial and ethnic diversity in nonresident father involvement. *Journal of Marriage and Family, 66,* 1–21.

King, V., & Heard, H. E. (1999). Nonresident father visitation, parental conflict, and mother's satisfaction: What's best for child well-being? *Journal of Marriage and the Family, 61,* 385–396.

Kirschner, B. F., & Walum, L. M. (1978). Two-location families. *Alternative Lifestyles, 1,* 513–525.

Kissman, K. (1997). Noncustodial fatherhood: Research trends and issues. *Journal of Divorce and Remarriage, 28,* 77–88.

Knapp, M. L., Daly, J. A., Albada, K., & Miller, G. R. (2002). Background and current trends in the study of interpersonal communication. In M. L. Knapp & J. A. Daly (Eds.), *Handbook of interpersonal communication* (pp. 2–30). Thousands Oaks, CA: Sage.

Knoester, C. (2003). Transitions in young adulthood and the relationship between parent and offspring well-being. *Social Forces, 81,* 1431–1458.

Knox, J., & Price, D. H. (1995). The changing American military family: Opportunities for social work. *Social Service Review, 69,* 479–497.

Knox, D., Zusman, M. E., Daniels, V., & Brantley, A. (2002). Absence makes the heart grow fonder? Long distance dating relationships among college students. *College Student Journal, 36,* 364–367.

Koerner, A. F., & Fitzpatrick, M. A. (2002). Toward a theory of family communication. *Communication Theory, 12,* 70–91.

Koerner, A. F., & Fitzpatrick, M. A. (2004). Communication in intact families. In A. Vangelisti (Ed.), *The handbook of family communication* (pp. 177–195). Mahwah, NJ: Lawrence Erlbaum Associates.

Kot, L., & Shoemaker, H. M. (1999). Children of divorce: An investigation of the developmental effects from infancy through adulthood. *Journal of Divorce and Remarriage, 31,* 161–178.

Kraut, R., Kiesler, S., Boneva, B., Cummings, J., Helgeson, V., & Crawford, A. (2002). Internet paradox revisited. *Journal of Social Issues, 58,* 49–74.

Kraut, R., Lundmark, V., Patterson, M., Kiesler, S., Mukopadhyay, T., & Scherlis, W. (1998). Internet paradox: A social technology that reduces social involvement and psychological well-being? *American Psychologist, 53*, 1017–1031.

Lamb, M. E. (1997). Fathers and child development: An introductory overview and guide. In M. E. Lamb (Ed.), *The role of the father in child development* (3rd ed., pp. 1–18). New York: Wiley.

Lapsley, D. K., Rice, K. G., & Fitzgerald, D. P. (1990). Adolescent attachment, identity, and adjustment to college: Implications for the continuity of adaptation hypothesis. *Journal of Counseling and Development, 68*, 561–565.

Larson, J. H., & Holman, T. B. (1994). Premarital predictors of marital quality and stability. *Family Relations, 43*, 228–237.

Le, B., & Agnew, C. R. (2001). Need fulfillment and emotional experience in interdependent romantic relationships. *Journal of Social and Personal Relationships, 18*, 423–440.

Lea, M., & Spears, R. (1995). Love at first byte? In J. T. Wood & S. W. Duck (Eds.), *Understudied relationships: Off the beaten track* (pp. 197–238). Thousand Oaks, CA: Sage.

Leeds-Hurwitz, W. S. (Ed.). (1995). *Social approaches to communication*. New York: Guilford.

Leite, R. W., & McKenry, P. C. (2002). Aspects of father status and post divorce father involvement with children. *Journal of Family Issues, 23*, 601–623.

Lenton, S. (2003). Policy from a harm reduction perspective. *Current Opinion in Psychiatry, 16*, 271–278.

Le Roux, T. (1995). *"We have families too." Live-in domestics talk about their lives.* Pretoria, South Africa: Human Sciences Research Council.

Levin, I., & Trost, J. (1999). Living together apart. *Community, Work, and Family, 2*, 279–292.

Lin, G., & Rogerson, P. A. (1995). Elderly parents and the geographic availability of their adult children. *Research on Aging, 17*, 303–331.

Lindholm, C. (1998). Love and structure. *Theory of Culture and Society, 15*, 215–241.

Litwak, E. (1985). *Helping the elderly: The complementary roles of informal and formal systems*. New York: Guilford.

Lorenz, K. Z. (1966). Evolution of ritualization in the biological and cultural spheres. In J. Huxley (Ed.), *A discussion on ritualization of behaviour in animals and man: Philosophical Transactions of the Royal Society of London Series B* (Vol. 259, pp. 273–284). Royal Society.

Lowenstein, A. (1986). Temporary single parenthood: The case of prisoner's families. *Family Relations, 35*, 79–85.

Luescher, K., & Pillemer, K. (1998). Intergenerational ambivalence: A new approach to the study of parent–child relations in later life. *Journal of Marriage and the Family, 60*, 413–425.

Lydon, J., Pierce, T., & O'Regan, S. (1997). Coping with moral commitment to long-distance dating relationships. *Journal of Personality and Social Psychology, 73*, 104–113.

Lye, D. J. (1996). Adult child–parent relationships. *Annual Review of Sociology, 22,* 79–102.

Lynd, R. S., & Lynd, H. M. (1929). *The demise of Littletown.* New York: Harcourt, Brace.

Magnuson, S., & Norem, K. (1999). Challenges of higher-education couples in commuter marriages: Insights for couples and counselors who work with them. *The Family Journal, 7,* 125–134.

Maines, J. (1993). Long-distance romances. *American Demographics, 15,* 47.

Mares, M. (1995). The aging family. In M. A. Fitzpatrick & A. L. Vangelisti (Eds.), *Explaining family interactions* (pp. 344–374). Thousand Oaks, CA: Sage.

Martin, J., & McClure, P. (2000). Today's active duty military family: The evolving challenges of military family life. In J. A. Martin, L. N. Rosen, & L. R. Sparacino (Eds.), *The military family, a practice guide for human service providers* (pp. 3–23). Westport, CO: Praeger.

Masuda, M., & Duck, S. W. (2002). Issues in ebb and flow: Management and maintenance of relationships as a skilled activity. In J. S. Harvey & A. Wenzel (Eds.), *Maintaining and enhancing close relationships* (pp. 13–41). Mahwah, NJ: Lawrence Erlbaum Associates.

McCubbin, H. I., Dahl, B. B., Lester, G. R., Benson, D., & Robertson, M. L. (1976). Coping repertoires of families adapting to prolonged war-induced separations. *Journal of Marriage and the Family, 38,* 461–471.

McEntee, M. (2003, December 11). Movement of forces into Iraq in next few months will slow R&R program. *Stars and Stripes.* Retrieved December 11, 2003 from http://www.estripes.com

McGhee, J. L. (1985). The effects of siblings on the life satisfaction on the rural elderly. *Journal of Marriage and Family, 47,* 85–91.

McKenna, K. Y. A., & Bargh, J. A. (2000). Plan 9 from cyberspace: The implications of the Internet for personality and social psychology. *Personality and Social Psychology Review, 4,* 57–75.

McKenna, K. Y. A., Green, A. S., & Gleason, M. J. (2002). Relationships formation on the Internet: What's the big attraction? *Journal of Social Issues, 58,* 9–32.

McNeil, L., & Sher, M. (1999). The dual-career-couple problem. *Physics Today, 52,* 32–37.

Mead, G. H. (1934). *Mind, self, and society: From the standpoint of a social behaviorist.* Chicago: University of Chicago Press.

Messman, S. J., Canary, D. J., & Hause, K. S. (2000). Motives to remain platonic, equity, and the use of maintenance strategies in opposite-sex friendships. *Journal of Social and Personal Relationships, 17,* 67–94.

Meyers, S. A. (2001). Relational maintenance behaviors in the sibling relationship. *Communication Quarterly, 49,* 19–34.

Milardo, R. M., & Helms-Erikson, H. (2000). Close relationships: A source book. In C. Hendrick & S. Hendrick (Eds.), *Network overlap and third-party influence in close relationships* (pp. 33–45). Thousand Oaks, CA: Sage.

Military Family Resource Center. (2002). *Profile of the military community: 2001 demographics.* Retrieved June 20, 2004, from http://www.mfrc-dodqol.org

Miller, G. R., & Parks, M. R. (1982). Personal relationships: Dissolving personal relationships. In S. W. Duck (Ed.), *Communication in dissolving relationships* (Vol. 4, pp. 127–154). London: Academic Press.

Miller, P., Caughlin, J. P., & Huston, T. L. (2003). Trait expressiveness and marital satisfaction: The role of idealization processes. *Journal of Marriage and Family, 65,* 978–995.

Mills, T. L. (2001). Research on grandparent and grandchild relationships in the new millennium: An overview of the special issue. *Journal of Family Issues, 22,* 403–406.

Miner, S., & Uhlenberg, P. (1997). Intragenerational proximity and the social role of sibling neighbors after midlife. *Family Relations, 46,* 145–253.

Montgomery, B. M. (1993). Relationship maintenance versus relationship change: A dialectical dilemma. *Journal of Social and Personal Relationships, 10,* 205–224.

Morrice, J. K. W., & Taylor, J. C. (1978). The intermittent husband syndrome. *New Society, 43,* 12–13.

Mumola, C. J. (2000). *Bureau of Justice statistics special report: Incarcerated parents and their children.* Washington, DC: Department of Justice, Office of Justice Programs.

Murdock, G. P. (1949). *Social structure.* New York: Macmillan.

Murray, S. L., & Holmes, J. G. (1996). The construction of relationship realities. In G. J. O. Fletcher & J. Fitness (Eds.), *Knowledge structures in close relationships: A social psychological approach* (pp. 91–120). Mahwah, NJ: Lawrence Erlbaum Associates.

Murray, S. L., Holmes, J. G., & Griffen, D. W. (1996). The benefits of illusions: Idealization and the construction of satisfaction in close relationships. *Journal of Personality and Social Psychology, 70,* 79–98.

National Council of Family Relations. (2004). Building strong military families. Retrieved June 29, 2004, from www.ncfr.org/pdf/NCFR_New_PMS2.pdf.

Neugebauer, R. (1989). Divorce, custody, and visitation: The child's point of view. *Journal of Divorce, 12,* 153–168.

Nord, C. W., & Zill, N. (1996). *Non-custodial parents' participation in their children's lives: Evidence from the survey of income and program participation.* Final report prepared for the Office of the Assistant Secretary for Planning and Evaluation, U.S. Department of Health and Human Services.

Norwood, A. E., Fullerton, C. S., & Hagen, K. P. (1996). Those left behind: Military families. In R. J. Ursano & A. E. Norwood (Eds.), *Emotional aftermath of the Persian Gulf War: Veterans, families, communities, and nations* (pp. 163–196). Washington, DC: American Psychiatric Press.

Nurse, A. M. (2002). *Fatherhood arrested: Parenting from within the Juvenile Justice System.* Vanderbilt, TN: Vanderbilt University Press.

Nussbaum, J. F. (1994). Friendship in older adulthood. In M. L. Hummert & C. F. Nussbaum (Eds.), *Interpersonal communication in older adulthood: Interdisciplinary theory and research* (pp. 209–225). Thousand Oaks, CA: Sage.

Nussbaum, J. F., & Bettini, L. M. (1994). Shared stories of the grandparent–grandchild relationship. *International Journal of Aging and Human Development, 39,* 67–80.

O'Sullivan, P. (2000). What you don't know won't hurt me: Impression management functions of communication channels in relationships. *Human Communication Research, 26,* 403–431.

Oswald, D. L., & Clark, E. M. (2003). Best friends forever?: High school best friendships and the transition to college. *Personal Relationships, 10,* 187–196.

Parker, M. W., Vaughn, R. A. C., Dunkle, R., & Vaitkus, M. (2002). "Out of sight" but not "out of mind": Parent contact and worry among senior ranking male officers in the military who live long distances from parents. *Military Psychology, 14,* 257–277.

Parks, M. R. (1982). Ideology in interpersonal communication: Off the couch and into the world. In M. Burgoon (Ed.), *Communication yearbook 5* (pp. 79–108). New Brunswick, NJ: Transaction Books.

Parks, M. R. (1995). Ideology in interpersonal communication: Beyond the couches, talk shows, and bunkers. In B. R. Burleson (Ed.), *Communication yearbook 18* (pp. 480–497). Thousand Oaks, CA: Sage.

Parks, M. R., & Floyd, K. (1996). Making friends in cyberspace. *Journal of Communication. 46,* 80–97.

Parks, M. R., & Roberts, L. D. (1998). "Making MOOsic": The development of personal relationships on-line and comparison to their off-line counterparts. *Journal of Social and Personal Relationships, 15,* 517–537.

Parsons, T. (1965). The normal American family. In F. Farber, P. Mustacchi, & R. Wilson (Eds.), *Man and civilization* (pp. 31–50). New York: McGraw-Hill.

Perlman, D. (2001). Maintaining and enhancing relationships: Concluding commentary. In J. Harvey & A. Wenzel (Eds.), *Close romantic relationships: Preservation and enhancement* (pp. 357–378). Mahwah, NJ: Lawrence Erlbaum Associates.

Pew Internet & American Life Project. (2000a). *Tracking online life: How women use the Internet to cultivate relationships with family and friends.* Retrieved February 21, 2004, from http://www.pewinternet.org/reports/toc.asp?Report=11

Pew Internet & American Life Project. (2000b). *Trust and privacy online: Why Americans want to rewrite the rules.* Retrieved February 21, 2004, from http://www.pewinternet. org/reports/pdfs/PIP_Trust_Privacy_Report.pdf

Pew Internet & American Life Project. (2001a). *The commons of the tragedy: How the Internet was used by millions after the terror attacks to grieve, console, share news, and debate the country's response.* Retrieved February 21, 2004, from http://www.pewinternet. org/reports/toc.asp?Report=46

Pew Internet & American Life Project. (2001b). *Teenage life online: The rise of the instant-message generation and the Internet's impact on friendships and family relationships.* Retrieved from http://www.pewinternet.org/reports/toc.asp?Report=36

Pew Internet & American Life Project. (2003). *America's online pursuits: The changing picture of who's online and what they do.* Retrieved February 21, 2004, from http://www. pewinternet.org/reports/toc.asp?Report=106

Pew Internet & American Life Project. (2004a). *Older Americans and the Internet.* Retrieved June 30, 2004, from www.pewinternet.org/PPF/c/2/topics.asp

Pew Internet & American Life Project. (2004b). *Tracking surveys (March 2000–present)*. Retrieved February 16, 2004, from http://www.pewinternet.org/reports/chart.asp?img=Daily_Activities_1.14.04.htm.

Pierce, P. F., Vinokur, A. D., & Buck, C. L. (1998). Effects of war-induced maternal separation on children's adjustment during the Gulf War and two years later. *Journal of Applied Social Psychology, 28*, 1286–1311.

Pincus, S. H., House, R., Christenson, J., & Adler, L. E. (2001). The emotional cycle of deployment: A military family perspective. *U.S. Army Medical Department Journal, 4/5/6*, 15–23.

Pincus, S. H., & Nam, T. A. (1999). Psychological aspects of deployment: The Bosnian experience. *Journal of the United States Army Medical Department, 1/2/3*, 38–44.

Pulakos, J. (1989). Young adult relationships: Siblings and friends. *Journal of Psychology, 12*, 237–244.

Rabby, M. K. (1997, November). *Maintaining relationships via electronic mail*. Paper presented at the annual meeting of the National Communication Association, Chicago.

Rabby, M. K., & Walther, J. B. (2003). Computer-mediated effects on relationship formation and maintenance. In D. J. Canary & M. Dainton (Eds.), *Maintaining relationships through communication: Relational, contextual, and cultural variations* (pp. 141–162). Mahwah, NJ: Lawrence Erlbaum Associates.

Ramirez, A., Jr., & Broneck, K. (in press). "IM me": Instant messaging as relational maintenance and everyday communication. *Journal of Social and Personal Relationships*.

Ramirez,, A., Jr., Walther, J. B., Burgoon, J., & Sunnafrank, M. (2002). Information-seeking strategies, uncertainty, and computer mediated communication: Toward a conceptual model. *Human Communication Research, 28*, 317–348.

Rawlins, W. K. (1994). Being there and growing apart: Sustaining friendships during adulthood. In D. J. Canary & L. Stafford (Eds.), *Communication and relational maintenance* (pp. 275–294). New York: Academic Press.

Reed, B. J., & Segal, D. R. (2000). The impact of multiple deployments of soldiers' peacekeeping attitudes, morale, and retention. *Armed Forces and Society, 27*, 57–78.

Reed, D. F., & Reed, E. L. (1997). Children of incarcerated parents. *Social Justice, 24*, 152–169.

Reis, H. T., & Knee, C. R. (1996). What we know, what we don't know, and what we need to know about relationship knowledge structures. In G. J. O. Fletcher & J. Fitness (Eds.), *Knowledge structures in close relationships: A sociological approach* (pp. 169–191). Mahwah, NJ: Lawrence Erlbaum Associates.

Reske, J., & Stafford, L. (1989, May). *Idealization and communication in long-distance and geographically close premarital relationships*. Paper presented at the Annual Conference of the International Communication Association, San Francisco.

Reissman, C., Aron, A., & Bergen, M. R. (1993). Shared activities and marital satisfaction: Causal direction and self-expansion versus boredom. *Journal of Social and Personal Relationships, 10*, 243–454.

Rheingold, H. (1993). *The virtual community: Homesteading on the electronic frontier.* Reading, MA: Addison-Wesley.

Rhodes, A. R. (2002). Long-distance relationships in dual-career commuter couples: A review of counseling issues. *The Family Journal, 8,* 398–404.

Richmond, V. P. (1995). Amount of communication in marital dyads as a function of dyadic and individual marital satisfaction. *Communication Reports, 13,* 152–159.

Riley, M. W. (1983). The family in an aging society: A matrix of latent relationships. *Journal of Family Issues, 4,* 439–454.

Rindfuss, R. R., Chamratrithirong, A., & Morgan, S. P. (1988). Living arrangements and family formation. *Social Forces, 66,* 926–950.

Rindfuss, R. R., & Stephen, E. H. (1990). Marital noncohabitation: Separation does not make the heart grow fonder. *Journal of Marriage and the Family, 52,* 259–270.

Ritzer, G. (Ed.). (1992). *Metatheorizing.* Newbury Park, CA: Sage.

Roehling, P. V., & Bultman, M. (2002). Does absence make the heart grow fonder? Work-related travel and marital satisfaction. *Sex Roles, 46,* 279–293.

Rogers, E. (1998). The meaning of relationships in relational communication. In R. L. Conville & E. Rogers (Eds.), *The meaning of "relationship" in interpersonal communication* (pp. 69–82). Westport, CT: Praeger.

Rohall, D. E., Segal, M. W., & Segal, D. R. (1999). Examining the importance of organizational supports on family adjustment to Army life in a period of increasing separation. *Journal of Political and Military Sociology, 27,* 49–65.

Rohfling, M. (1995). "Doesn't anybody stay in one place anymore?" An exploration of the under-studied phenomenon of long-distance relationships. In J. Wood & S. W. Duck (Eds.), *Under-studied relationships: Off the beaten track* (pp. 173–196). Thousand Oaks, CA: Sage.

Roloff, M. E. (1981). *Interpersonal communication: The social exchange approach.* Beverly Hills, CA: Sage.

Rose, S. M., & Serefica, S. M. (1986). Keeping and ending casual, close, and best friendships. *Journal of Social and Personal Relationships, 11,* 275–288.

Rosen, L. N., Durand, D., Westhuis, D. J., & Teitelbaum, J. M. (1995). Marital adjustment of Army spouses one year after Operation Desert Storm. *Journal of Applied Social Psychology, 25,* 677–692.

Rosen, L. N., & Moghadam, L. Z. (1988). Social support, family separation, and well-being among military wives. *Behavioral Medicine, 14,* 64–70.

Rosenberg, G. S., & Anspach, D. F. (1973). Sibling solidarity in the working class. *Journal of Psychology, 12,* 237–244.

Ross, B. J. (2001). The emotional impact of e-mail on deployment. *Proceedings of the Naval Institute, 127,* 85–86.

Rossi, A., & Rossi, B. (1990). *Of human bonding: Relationships across the lifespan.* Hawthorne, NY: Aldine de Gruyter.

Rotter, J. C., Barnett, D. E., & Fawcett, M. L. (1998). On the road again: Dual-career commuter relationships. *The Family Journal, 6,* 46–49.

Rusbult, C. E. (1980). Commitment and satisfaction in romantic associations: A test of the investment model. *Journal of Experimental Social Psychology, 16,* 172–186.

Rusbult, C. E. (1983). A longitudinal test of the investment model: The development (and deterioration) of satisfaction and commitment in heterosexual involvements. *Journal of Personality and Social Psychology, 45*, 101–117.

Rusbult, C. E., Drigotas, S. M., & Verette, J. (1994). The investment model: An interdependence analysis of commitment processes and relationship maintenance phenomena. In D. J. Canary & L. Stafford (Eds.), *Communication and relational maintenance* (pp. 115–139). New York: Academic Press.

Rusbult, C. E., Olsen, N., Davis, J. L., & Hannon, P. A. (2001). Commitment and relationship maintenance mechanisms. In J. Harvey & A. Wenzel (Eds.), *Close romantic relationships*. Mahwah, NJ: Lawrence Erlbaum Associates.

Rusbult, C. E., Van Lange, P. A. M., Wildschut, T., Yovetich, A., & Verette, J. (2000). Perceived superiority in close relationships: Why it exists and persists. *Journal of Personality and Social Psychology, 79*, 521–545.

Sabatelli, R. M. (1988). Exploring relationship satisfaction: A social exchange perspective on the interdependence between theory, research, and practice. *Family Relations, 37*, 217–222.

Sahlstein, E. (2004). Relating at a distance: Negotiating being together and being apart in long-distance relationships. *Journal of Social and Personal Relationships, 21*, 698–201

Satir, V. (1988). *The new peoplemaking*. Mountain View, CA: Science and Behavior Books.

Scarr, S., & Gracek, S. (1992). Important variables in adult sibling relationships: A qualitative study. In M. E. Lamb & B. Sutton-Smith (Eds.), *Sibling relationships: Their nature and significance across the lifespan* (pp. 357–381). Hillsdale, NJ: Lawrence Erlbaum Associates.

Schmidley, D. (2003). *The foreign-born population in the United States: March 2002*. Washington, DC: U.S. Census Bureau.

Schulman, M. L. (1974). Idealization in engaged couples. *Journal of Marriage and Family, 36*, 139–147.

Schumm, W. R., Bell, D. B., & Knott, B. (2000). Factors associated with spouses moving away from their military installation during an overseas deployment. *Psychological Reports, 86*, 1275–1282.

Schumm, W. R., Bell, D. B., Knott, B., & Rice, R. E. (1996). The perceived effect of stressors on marital satisfaction among civilian wives of enlisted soldiers deployed to Somalia for Operation Restore Hope. *Military Medicine, 161*, 601–606.

Schutz, A. (1964). The homecomer. In A. Broderson (Ed.), *Collected papers* (Vol. 2, pp. 106–119). The Hague, Netherlands: Martinus Nijhoff.

Schwebel, A. I., Dunn, R. L., Moss, B. F., & Renner, M. A. (1992). Factors associated with relational stability in geographically separated couples. *Journal of College Student Development, 33*, 222–230.

Seefeldt, C., & Keawkungwal, S. (1986). Children's attitudes toward the elderly in Thailand. *Educational Gerontology, 12*, 151–158.

Segrin, C., & Flora, J. (2001). Perceptions of relational histories, marital quality, and loneliness when communication is limited: An examination of married prison inmates. *Journal of Family Communication, 1*, 151–174.

Seltzer, J. A. (1991). Relationships between fathers and children who live apart: The father's role after separation. *Journal of Marriage and Family, 53*, 79–101.

Seymour, C. (1998). Children with parents in prison: Child welfare policy, program, and practice issues. *Child Welfare, 77*, 469–493.

Sherrod, L. R. (1996). Leaving home: The role of individual and familial factors. *New Directions for Child Development, 71*, 111–119.

Shwalb, D. W., Imaizumi, N., & Nakazawa, J. (1987). The modern Japanese father: Roles and problems in a changing society. In M. E. Lamb (Ed.), *The father's role: Cross-cultural perspectives* (pp. 247–269). Hillsdale, NJ: Lawrence Erlbaum Associates.

Sigman, S. J. (1991). Handling the discontinuous aspects of continuing social relationships: Toward research on the persistence of social forms. *Communication Theory, 1*, 106–127.

Sigman, S. J. (1998). Relationships and communication: A social communication and strongly consequential view. In R. L. Conville & L. E. Rogers (Eds.), *The meaning of "relationship" in interpersonal communication* (pp. 47–68). Westport, CT: Praeger.

Sillars, A. L. (1998). (Mis)understanding. In B. H. Spitzberg & W. R. Cupach (Eds.), *The dark side of close relationships* (pp. 73–102). Mahwah, NJ: Lawrence Erlbaum Associates.

Silverstein, M., Lawton, L., & Bengston, V. L. (1994). Types of relations between parents and adult children. In V. L. Bengston & R. A. Harootyan (Eds.), *Intergenerational linkages* (pp. 43–76). New York: Springer.

Simpson, J., Ickes, W., & Blackstone, T. (1995). When the head protects the heart: Empathic accuracy in dating relationships. *Journal of Personality and Social Psychology, 69*, 629–641.

Smith, G. C. (1998). Residential separation and patterns of interaction between elderly parents and their adult children. *Progress in Human Geography, 22*, 368–384.

Smykla, J. O. (1987). The human impact of capital punishment: Interviews with families of persons on death row. *Journal of Criminal Justice, 15*, 331–346.

Snyder, Z. K., Carlo, T. A., & Coats, M. M. (2001). Parenting from prison: An examination of children's visitation programs at a women's correctional facility. *Marriage and Family Review, 32*, 33–61.

Spence, S. A., Black, S. R., Adams, J. P., & Crowther, M. R. (2001). Grandparents and grandparenting in a rural southern state: A study of demographic characteristics, roles, and relationships. *Journal of Family Issues, 22*, 523–534.

Spiro, M. E. (1954). Is the family universal? *American Anthropologist, 56*, 839–846.

Spitzberg, B. H., & Hoobler, G. (2002). Cyberstalking and the technologies of interpersonal terrorism. *New Media & Society, 4*, 71–92.

Sprecher, S. (1986). The relation between equity and emotions in close relationships. *Social Psychology Bulletin, 49*, 309–321.

Sprecher, S., & Felmlee, D. (2000). Romantic partners' perceptions of social network attributes with the passage of time and relationship transitions. *Personal Relationships, 7*, 325–340.

Sprecher, S., & Regan, P. C. (1998). Passionate and companionate love in courting and young married couples. *Sociological Inquiry, 68*, 163–185.

Stafford, L. (1994). Tracing the threads of spider webs. In D. J. Canary & L. Stafford (Eds.), *Communication and relational maintenance* (pp. 297–306). San Diego, CA: Academic Press.

Stafford, L. (2003). Maintaining romantic relationships: Summary and analysis of one research program. In D. J. Canary & M. Dainton (Eds.), *Maintaining relationships through communication* (pp. 59–78). Mahwah, NJ: Lawrence Erlbaum Associates.

Stafford, L. (2004, July). *Long-distance dating relationships: Are we asking the right questions?* Paper presented at the International Association for Relational Research, Madison, WI.

Stafford, L., & Bayer, C. L. (1993). *Interaction between parents and children.* Newbury Park, CA: Sage.

Stafford, L., & Canary, D. J. (1991). Maintenance strategies and romantic relationship type, gender, and relational characteristics. *Journal of Social and Personal Relationships, 8,* 217–242.

Stafford, L., Dainton, L., & Haas, S. M. (2000). Measuring routine and strategic relational maintenance: Scale revision, sex versus gender roles, and the prediction of relational characteristics. *Communication Monographs, 3,* 306–323.

Stafford, L., Kline, S., & Dimmick, J. (1999). Home e-mail: Relational maintenance and gratification opportunities. *Journal of Electronic and Broadcasting Media, 43,* 659–669.

Stafford, L., Merolla, A. J., & Castle, J. D. (2004). *When long-distance dating relationships become geographically close relationships.* Manuscript submitted for publication.

Stafford, L., & Reske, J. R. (1990). Idealization and communication in long-distance premarital relationships. *Family Relations, 39,* 274–279.

Stafford, L., & Yost, S. (1990, November). *The role of communication in naval couples' marital satisfaction.* Paper presented at the annual conference of the National Communication Association, Chicago.

Steiner, P. (1993, July 5). On the Internet no one knows you're a dog. *The New Yorker,* p. 63.

Stephen, T. (1986). Communication and interdependence in geographically separated relationships. *Human Communication Research, 13,* 191–210.

Sternberg, R. J., & Barnes, M. L. (1985). Real and ideal others in romantic relationships: Is four a crowd? *Journal of Personality and Social Psychology, 49,* 1586–1608.

Stewart, S. D. (2003). Nonresident parenting and adolescent adjustment. *Journal of Family Issues, 24,* 217–244.

Strawbridge, W. J., & Wallhagen, M. I. (1991). Impact of family conflict on adult-child caregivers. *Gerontologist, 31,* 770–777.

Stroh, L. K. (1999). A review of relocation: The impact on work and family. *Human Resource Management Review, 9,* 279–308.

Suarez, Z. E. (1998). Cuban-American families. In C. H. Mindel, R. W. Habenstein, & R. Wright Jr. (Eds.), *Ethnic families in America: Patterns and variations* (pp. 172–198). Upper Saddle River, NJ: Prentice Hall.

Sweet, J., Bumpass, L. L., & Call, V. (1988.). *The design and content of the national survey of families and households.* Madison: University of Wisconsin, Center for Demography and Ecology.

Taylor, A. S., & Lounsbury, J. W. (1988). Dual-career couples and geographic transfer: Executives' reactions to commuter marriage and attitude toward the move. *Human Relations, 47,* 407–424.

Taylor, S. E., & Brown, J. D. (1988). Illusions and well-being: A social-psychological perspective on mental health. *Psychology Bulletin, 21,* 32–44.

Thompson, S. J., Kost, K. A., & Pollio, D. E. (2003). Examining risk factors associated with family reunification for runaway youth: Does ethnicity matter? *Family Relations, 52,* 296–304.

Tidwell, L. C., & Walther, J. B. (2002). Computer mediated communication effects on disclosure, impressions, and personal evaluations: Getting to know one another one bit at a time. *Human Communication Research, 28,* 317–348.

Treas, J., & Lawton, L. (1999). Family relations in adulthood. In M. Sussman, S. K. Steinmetz, & G. W. Peterson (Eds.), *Handbook of marriage and the family* (2nd ed., pp. 425–438). New York: Plenum.

Trice, A. D. (2002). First semester college students' e-mail to parents: Frequency and content related to parenting style. *College Student Journal, 36,* 327.

Uhlenberg, P., & Hammill, B. G. (1998). Frequency of grandparent contact with grandchild sets: Six factors that make a difference. *The Gerontologist, 38,* 276–285.

Ursano, R. J., & Norwood, A. E. (1996). *Emotional aftermath of the Persian Gulf War: Veterans, families, communities and nations.* Washington, DC: American Psychiatric Press.

U.S. Census Bureau. (2002). *Current population survey (CPS): Definitions and explanations.* Retrieved August 2, 2003, from http://www.census.gov/population/www/cps/cpsdef.html.

U.S. Presidential Commission. (1993). *Women in combat: Report to the president.* Washington, DC: Brassey's.

Van Breda, A. D. (1999). Developing resilience to routine separations: An occupational social work intervention. *Families in Society: The Journal of Contemporary Human Services, 80,* 597–605.

VanderVoort, L. A., & Duck, S. W. (2000). Talking about relationships: Variations on a theme. In K. Dindia & S. W. Duck (Eds.), *Communication and personal relationships* (pp. 1–12). Chichester, England: Wiley.

Vangelisti, A. (2002). Interpersonal processes in romantic relationships. In M. L. Knapp & J. A. Daly (Eds.), *Handbook of interpersonal communication* (3rd ed., pp. 643–679). Thousand Oaks, CA: Sage.

Vangelisti, A. L., & Banski, M. (1993). Couples' debriefing conversations: The impact of gender, occupation, and demographic characteristics. *Family Relations, 42,* 149–157.

VanHorn, K. R., Arnone, A., Nesbitt, K., Desilets, L., Sears, T., Griffin, M., & Brudi, R. (1997). Physical distance and interpersonal characteristics in college students' romantic relationships. *Personal Relationships, 4,* 25–34.

Vela, A. M., & Lee, B. (Eds.). (2001). *Migrant and seasonal hired adolescent farmworkers.* Marsfield, WI: Marsfield Clinic.

Viljoen, S. (1994). *Strengths and weaknesses in the family life of black South Africans.* Pretoria, South Africa: Human Sciences Research Center.

Vogl-Baeur, S. (2003). Maintaining family relationships. In D. J. Canary & M. Dainton (Eds.), *Maintaining relationships through communication: Relational, contextual and cultural variations* (pp. 31–50). Mahwah, NJ: Lawrence Erlbaum Associates.

Vogl-Bauer, S., Kalbfleisch, P. J., & Beatty, M. J. (1999). Perceived equity, satisfaction, and relational maintenance strategies in parent–adolescent dyads. *Journal of Youth and Adolescence, 28,* 27–49.

Vormbrock, J. K. (1993). Attachment theory as applied to wartime and job-related marital separation. *Psychological Bulletin, 114,* 122–144.

Waller, W. (1938). *The family.* New York: Holt.

Waller, W. (1940). *War and the family.* New York: Dryden.

Walster (Hatfield), E., Berscheid, E., & Walster, G. W. (1973). New directions in equity research. *Journal of Personality and Social Psychology, 25,* 151–176.

Walther, J. B. (1992). Interpersonal effects in computer-mediated interaction: A relational perspective. *Communication Research, 19,* 52–90.

Walther, J. B. (1994). Anticipated ongoing interaction versus channel effects on relational communication in computer-mediated interaction. *Human Communication Research, 20,* 473–501.

Walther, J. B., Anderson, J. F., & Parks, D. (1994). Interpersonal effects in computer mediated interaction: A meta-analysis of social and antisocial communication. *Communication Research, 21,* 450–487.

Walther, J. B., & D'Addario, K. P. (2001). The impacts of emoticons on message interpretation in computer-mediated communication. *Social Science Computer Review, 19,* 323–345.

Walther, J. B., & Parks, M. (2002). Cues filtered out, cues filtered in: Computer-mediated communication and relationships. In M. L. Knapp & J. A. Daly (Eds.), *Handbook of interpersonal communication* (3rd ed., pp. 529–563). Thousand Oaks, CA: Sage.

Walther, J. B., Slovacek, C., & Tidwell, L. C. (2001). Is a picture worth 1000 words?: Photographic images in long-term and short-term virtual teams. *Communication Research, 28,* 105–134.

Walther, J. B., & Tidwell, L. C. (1995). Nonverbal cues in computer-mediated communication, and the effect of chronemics on relational communication. *Journal of Organizational Computing, 5,* 355–378.

Wamboldt, F. S., & Reiss, D. (1989). Defining a family heritage and a new relationship identity: Two central tasks in the making of a marriage. *Family Process, 28,* 317–335.

Watzlawick, P., Beavin, J. H., & Jackson, D. D. (1967). *Pragmatics of human communication.* New York: Norton.

Wellman, B. (1999). The network community: An introduction. In B. Wellman (Ed.), *Networks in the global community* (pp. 1–47). Boulder, CO: Westview.

Wellman, B., & Wortley, S. (1989). Brothers' keepers: Situating kinship relations in broader networks of social support. *Sociological Perspectives, 32,* 273–306.

Wendel, W. C. (1975). High school sweethearts: A study in separation and commitment. *Journal of Clinical Child Psychology, 4,* 45–46.

Westefeld, J. S., & Liddell, D. (1982). Coping with long-distance relationships. *Journal of College Student Development, 23*, 550–551.

Western, B., & McLanahan, S. (2000). Fathers behind bars: The impact of incarceration on family formation. *Contemporary Perspectives in Family Fesearch, 2*, 307–322.

Whitbeck, L. B., Hoyt, D. R., & Ackley, K. A. (1997). Abuseive family backgrounds and later victimization among runaway and homeless adolesence. *Journal of Research on Adolescence, 7*, 375–392.

White, L. (1994). Coresidence and leaving home: Young adults and their parents. *Annual Review of Sociology, 20*, 81–201.

White, L. K. (2001). Sibling relationships over the life course: A panel analysis. *Journal of Marriage and the Family, 63*, 555–568.

White, L. K., & Riedmann, A. (1992a). Ties among adult siblings. *Social Forces, 71*, 85–102.

White, L. K., & Riedmann, A. (1992b). When the Brady Bunch grows up: Step/half- and fullsibling relationships in adulthood. *Journal of Marriage and the Family, 54*, 197–208.

Williams, A., & Nussbaum, J. F. (2001). *Intergenerational communication across the life span.* Mahwah, NJ: Lawrence Erlbaum Associates.

Wilmot, W. W. (1995). *Relational communication.* New York: McGraw-Hill.

Wilmot, W. W., & Carbaugh, D. (1986). Long-distance lovers: Predicting the dissolution of relationships. *Journal of Northwest Communication Association, 14*, 43–59.

Winfield, F. E. (1985). *Commuter marriage: Living together, apart.* New York: Columbia University Press.

Wolchik, S. A., Fenaughty, A. M., & Braver, S. L. (1996). Residential and nonresidential parents' perspectives on visitation problems. *Family Relations, 45*, 230–237.

Wood, J. T., & Duck, S. (Eds.). (1995). *Under-studied relationships: Off the beaten path.* Thousand Oaks, CA: Sage.

Wood, S., Scarville, J., & Gravino, K. S. (1995). Waiting wives: Separation and reunion among Army wives. *Armed Forces and Society, 21*, 217–236.

Wright, P. H. (1984). Self-referent motivation and the intrinsic quality of friendship. *Journal of Social and Personal Relationships, 1*, 115–130.

Author Index

Note: *n* indicates footnote.

A

Subject Index

Note: *t* indicates table.

Lightning Source UK Ltd.
Milton Keynes UK
UKHW042103250219
338016UK00010B/121/P